ART is for Everyone

by Martha Simpson

MARTHA SIMPSON

Martha Simpson was born and received her early education in Chicago, Illinois. After completing her formal schooling, she studied at the Chicago Art Institute for four and a half years and l'Académie André Lhôte, in Paris, for two. She has exhibited her paintings in art shows all over the United States, has taught art in several Western schools, and has done extensive work in ceramics.

In her twenty years as a practicing artist Miss Simpson has often noticed the hunger to understand and appreciate good art that many Americans carry around with them, unfulfilled, all their lives. She believes the reason for this unhappy situation is the popular distrust and fear of the abstract "highbrow" language that too often surrounds the subject of art. ART IS FOR EVERYONE was written to fill the need for a straightforward, nontechnical approach to art of the past and present and to prove that art criticism can be intelligent without being wordy.

Robert Beverly Hale, the Associate Curator of American Art for The Metropolitan Museum of Art in New York City, says of Miss Simpson's book—"ART IS FOR EVERYONE explains with the greatest clarity the forces that compel the contemporary artist to paint the way he does. I have yet to read a book on this subject that contains less nonsense."

ART IS FOR EVERYONE

MARTHA SIMPSON

art
is for
everyone

McGraw-Hill Book Company, Inc.

New York   London   Toronto

4892

ART IS FOR EVERYONE

Published by the McGraw-Hill Book Company, Inc.
Printed in the United States of America

To *William Derry Eastlake*

CONTENTS

FOREWORD

The English critic Clive Bell once remarked somewhere that though most people readily admit that they understand very little about music, nearly everybody considers himself entitled to an opinion about art. And a very generally held opinion about the art of the past fifty years is that it is, as a whole, cryptic, perverse, "modern," and very confusing. This, of course, is not at all surprising. A great many things have happened to art during the first half of our century, and the enormous variety of techniques developed by artists during this period—the apparently endless and conflicting avenues through which they have approached their aesthetic problems —are apt to strike the average man, who gives a hurried look at the end product, as bewildering indeed. Yet if one takes the trouble to find out what the artist is doing and to ask one-self a few really searching questions about what aspects of art one really values, it turns out that the confusion is not in the mind of today's artist but in the mind of today's layman, who has simply not thought enough about art to distinguish that which is aesthetically meaningful from that which is more or less irrelevant to aesthetic enjoyment. Actually, it takes a great deal of looking and a great deal of thinking before the average person is prepared to make these distinctions and to qualify as one who really understands art. Prejudices must be broken down; new ways of seeing must be cultivated. The process is one of mental and spiritual enrichment. But to carry it out, a guiding hand is needed.

In this book, Martha Simpson, herself a distinguished American painter, has provided such a guiding hand. And though her reasoning reflects both a profound knowledge of art and much patient analysis of her craft, it is expressed with such clarity that almost anyone can understand and profit by what she has to say. Art today probably reflects a broader and more comprehensive view of aesthetics than has ever before existed in history. Modern historical scholarship has acquainted us with the artistic products of many civilizations and eras which our forefathers ignored. Modern anthropology and psychology, the invention of the camera, the changing function of art in relation to human needs, have all profoundly affected the work of the artist. Yet they have not really affected the fundamental meaning, or message, of art, which remains universal and has been expressed quite similarly by artists as far apart in history as those of modern France, those of the Italian Renaissance, and those who painted the neolithic animals on the cave walls of prehistoric Dordogne. To appreciate this message demands, for most of us, a process of reeducation in which we throw aside our provincial preconceptions and seek an understanding of the basic values that are common to all art. In so doing, we enter a new world of visual experience which, though new to us, is really one of the oldest and most universal areas in which men have communicated their ideas and emotions. I hope that many readers will find in this volume a doorway into this world.

WINTHROP SARGEANT

ART IS FOR EVERYONE

1

WHERE DOES ART COME FROM AND WHERE IS IT GOING?

Art is for everyone. Not only for the rich collector, not only for the man with special knowledge of an esoteric mystery, but for you and for me. Whether we realize it or not, art has had an influence in making us what we are. It should be and can be a living part of the lives of all of us. It can be understood by everyone. It belongs to us all; it is our heritage; and if we do not come into this inherited wealth that is waiting for us, that is ours for the taking, we are missing much that will make our lives pleasanter and more exciting.

What is needed to enable us to come into this inheritance? To ask the right questions. We are curious about so many things. We ask so many questions in science, in history, in philosophy. Let us try to ask the questions about art that will open for us what has been called the third eye, the inner eye.

If knowledge can open for us this third eye, we are tempted to ask quickly, "What is art?" But in our search for the meaning of art it would be helpful to ask first an easier question than "What is art?" Let us ask, "Where did art come from? Where has it thrived? When and under what circumstances has it best manifested itself?"

To begin with we shall have to take a short glance back through history and have a look at the origin and development of art in the past in relation to the men who produced it and to the countries and civilizations in which it has become dominant at different times. It simplifies matters for us that most of the art that has survived the centuries is good art; that is, we can be sure that it corresponds to some inner need of man in general and not of just one particular period. The works of art that do not have a timeless and universal appeal, those that pleased man at only one time and place or under certain unique conditions, have mostly found their way to the cellars and dust heaps or have been put on dusty shelves in their rightful place among historical curiosities. Time and the needs of men have, for the most part, winnowed the wheat from the chaff.

But sometimes when anthropologists dig up the remains of old civilizations, they find preserved the good and the bad together, a real cross-section of all the works of men that happened to be preserved simply by chance, not by enduring merit. All these things find their way into museums and are lumped together as works of art. Even in the far remote ages of history there were false artists. There is a Persian sacrificial bowl so carelessly and haphazardly done that it is painful to see. All the traditional elements of de-

2

sign are there—the god portrayed on the side of the bowl, the decorative bands, the ornaments—but put together without love or feeling just to get the job done and probably with an eye on the pay. The bowl tells us the state of the artist's mind as plainly as though the bowl had been fashioned in New York yesterday instead of 4,000 years ago in Persia.

There are works of art produced by artists who were not attuned to their own period, whose message and meaning only became clear to later generations. There are whole schools of art—for example, the Byzantine and the Greek —whose value, while understood and appreciated by their own contemporaries, became obscured and meaningless to following generations, and was rediscovered when the psychological and social conditions again became favorable, when the emotional message again was needed. In the centuries, the millenniums, of man's history on earth, incalculable numbers of works of art have been produced. Some have been lost to us for all time; some have been temporarily lost and rediscovered, like the Mayan; some have fallen into disrepute and temporary obscurity. Today the impressionists, men such as Pissaro and Monet, seem to be losing their meaning for us. Perhaps they will be revived by future generations. As archeological research goes on, more works of art are coming to light. The history of mankind's creative activity is continuous, but the story of individual and racial production of art objects is complicated, and even now we have only the general outline. The details are fairly clear only for the last few hundred years, a mere second of archeological time. And the outlines of even this moment of art history are changing as our value judgments, influenced by our social conditions, change, and as lost or mislaid works of art come to light. If we look back over this record, faulty

3

as it is, it may be suggestive in helping us to answer some questions about the nature of art and our relation to art.

Standing here in the middle of the twentieth century is like standing on a high mountain. We can look back down the long vista of the past and trace the pattern that man has made by his activities, the rise and fall of civilizations, like mountain peaks, appearing now here, now there. The patterns are rich and varied, and among the most persistent of the patterns of man's activity appears the creative impulse.

Away back in the mists on the faintest horizon, where man begins to emerge into our view, are the first signs that he has left for us—the animal drawings in the caves of Spain and southern France. These were done in prehistoric times, long, long before any other record of man's handiwork, and show clearly that to create art was one of the first activities of the race. Early as these drawings were done —and they were done so long ago that no one can guess the exact period within a few thousand years—they show a technical proficiency that must have been acquired through many generations, indicating that even they were not the first. It seems that man turns to creating art as soon as he has made certain of staying alive and of keeping the race alive. (See Plate I.)

From those far horizons, where we first get a mysterious glimpse of man, our eye can follow the great art movements through the ages. These, like civilizations, rise like hills out of the plain. Each movement consists of a slope upwards, a peak or plateau, and a slope downwards. Some slope up abruptly to a sharp peak, and the decline is short and steep; some rise slowly to a long plateau and decline slowly. Sometimes there is only one movement, sometimes two or more at a time in different parts of the world. And we can see that the high points of civilization and high points of art are

4

sometimes together and sometimes separate. Sometimes the highest point of an art movement comes well on the downward slope of a civilization, sometimes on the way up.

After the cave drawings there is a long period which is a blank to us. No doubt, man was creating works of art during this period, but they are lost. Works of art appear again in Babylonia and Assyria; this is the first recorded movement. But art, when we first know it through existing works, is already sophisticated and shows a long period of development and tradition. It is stylized and symbolical, not naive and spontaneous. It takes a long time to develop styles and symbols; they are not invented by one artist but by an enduring school. By *school* is meant a group of artists working in, and adding to, a tradition of particular art theories; and in a *movement* there may be one or many schools.

, The next great rise of art occurred in Egypt. Here is the longest, most sustained art movement in history, lasting from 3500 b.c. almost to the present day, indeed up to the last century, with some periods of greater or less decline and some periods of minor change. For thousands of years this art maintained a high and equal standard with rigidly set traditions, which, in spite of being fairly inflexible, did not deteriorate. The reasons for this continuity may be that the Egyptian political system was stable, that there were no major changes in men's lives, and that art was in the hands of the educated, priestly class, who devoted their lives to it and were well trained in it from generation to generation. This tradition limited the originality of the individual and robbed the art of the infusion of new ideas, but at the same time kept the art from deteriorating from the established level. The art was highly stylized, flat, and decorative. There was no great change in this art until the spread of the Christian religion in the sixth century

5

brought new ideas and new ways of life. The Egyptians assimilated these to their old traditions and created a new and vital art form, the Coptic, firmly grafted on the old art, but freer and more living.

While Egyptian art was flourishing, art in Persia was rising. We have fine examples of Persian art made by some potter about 4,000 years before Christ; that is, about 6,000 years ago! These pieces are not crude beginnings, but finished works of art that show a long previous history. Art was probably thriving in Persia in 5000 B.C. Persian art is one of the greatest and most important arts in history, not only because it, like the Egyptian, is one of the most enduring—it, too, survived many vicissitudes and lost its vitality only in the last century—but also because of its influence on other countries and other arts. Every nation that came into contact with the Persians, by conquering or being conquered by them, was influenced in its art to such an extent that the art became Persian. No matter who won the battle, Persian art was always the victor.

The infiltration of Persia by the Arabs spread Persian art all over the then known world. The Arabs came out of an artistic vacuum, with no styles of their own to impose, and they were in control of the world from China to Gibraltar. They were wealthy and powerful, and they recognized the ability of the Persian artists and sent them to all the outposts of the Islamic empire to produce and teach art. We can see the strong Persian influence in Spanish art, in the art of North Africa, and even in the work of some artists in Europe today, notably Matisse. (See Plate XXI.) There has probably never been a group of men so sensitive, so creative, working in a tradition that sustained, but did not limit them. The examples of Persian art that are most typical and

6

that spring immediately to mind are the delicate, sensitive miniature paintings in water color.

About 2000 B.C. farther to the east, the great slope of Chinese art begins to arise. Here, too, for thousands of years men produced great and enduring art. In the slope we can distinguish undulations—there are several peaks and slight declines—but an amazingly high level of art has been maintained, nourished by a rich tradition, almost up to our own day.

One of these peaks is what is known as the Han period, which lasted for roughly four hundred years, from about 200 B.C. to A.D. 200. When we look at a Han figurine, it seems as modern as though it had been modeled yesterday. These figures are warm and human and touching. We know that those Chinese sculptors thought and felt as we think and feel. (See Plate I.)

Another great period was the T'ang, from the seventh to the tenth century A.D. A curious thing about this period is that it had a strong relationship to European Gothic art, although no direct influence is possible. The likeness is an example of two peoples going through a similar phase, though separated in time and in geography. (See Plate I.)

We must not leave the art of China without noting its influence on Japanese art and, through that, on European art. Many European artists of the last century were much influenced by Japanese prints. The most obvious example of such influence is Whistler. Probably even now, after 4,000 years of continuous art activity, the Chinese would still be fabricating fine works of art if the unsettling conditions of war did not prevent the artists from working.

About 600 B.C. we see a peak spring suddenly out of the plain, attain a towering height, and disappear, but not before its influence had spread over the whole civilized world. This peak is Greek art, and strong traces of it affect our thinking about art even today. Through the conquests of Alexander, this art was spread throughout Asia, Tunisia, and Egypt and had a humanizing and revitalizing influence on the rather static art of these countries.

Greek traditions and ideas were taken over whole by the Romans, whose culture rose when the Greek declined, and were modified by the practical, matter-of-fact Romans to fit their own personalities and needs. Roman art never rose to the pure heights of Greek art. These people harnessed art to utilitarian ends, where it never thrives well, and turned out realistic portrait busts to flatter the ego and accentuate the importance of the sitter, or adapted art to the decoration of public buildings and monuments to the glory of man or the state. Some of the portrait busts are quite beautiful, but they interest us more because they show us how particular people looked than as works of art in themselves. This art became more and more decadent until, about A.D. 200, a new spirit began to ferment among the people, a reaction against the materialism of the Roman culture, and this spirit manifested itself in the Christian religion and in art.

It is very interesting to watch this grow, at first literally underground, where the early Christians were driven to meet and worship by the persecution of the government in power, and then to see it spread gradually until the reign of Constantine, who officially adopted Christianity. This early Christian and Byzantine art is characterized by a broad, flat, powerful treatment. Its simplicity, strength, and management of flat surfaces endear it to many modern artists. (See Plate II.) During this period the rise of Christianity went hand in hand with the development of a new and

8

more spiritual art, which came to a full expression in the Byzantine period, when the Roman Empire itself had dwindled to a small territory around Constantinople. Here is an example of a great and powerful art thriving in a weak civilization, at the end of a long slope of political and military importance. The reason for this situation seems to be that, with the new ideas and spirit infused in the people, the energy that had been used to conquer and civilize was turned to the production of works of art.

This art seeped across Europe. Even in those times of slow transportation there were no boundaries to art and ideas. In France we find the Byzantine influence in the Romanesque churches, with their simple, strong sculpture, and in England we find it in the Norman architecture. In both these countries it was adapted to the different racial characters and individual personalities of the people. In the Romanesque sculpture the French humor, fantasy, and love of nature are clearly shown; in England the sculpture was subordinated to the architecture, which expressed the Englishman's love of clarity, stability, and logic.

In Europe the period from the decline of the Byzantine up to the rise of the Gothic in the twelfth century has long been called the Dark Ages. Social and economic conditions were appalling; life was uncertain. There was so little stability and security that it took most of man's time to solve the problem of staying alive, and little time or energy remained for the production of works of art. This picture of the Dark Ages, though true on the whole, is being modified a little as we become more familiar with the architecture (Romanesque and Norman), the funerary brasses, and the illuminated manuscripts which were produced in monasteries sheltered from the vicissitudes and insecurities of the life of the time. Strangely enough, it was during this period that

Ireland had its only period of art production. Its illuminated manuscripts, notably the Book of Kells, were vital and creative.

Then, about the middle of the twelfth century in France we suddenly see another, very abrupt, slope upwards. Why this movement should have arisen at this time and place is hard to see clearly, but again the rise of art was simultaneous with a revival of religious fervor. This time the shove forward was a gain in technical knowledge, the discovery of the broken arch and flying buttress in architecture. This discovery enabled men to raise the height of buildings, which had always been limited by the weight the walls could bear. Now the cathedrals shot up to towering heights, the roof weight distributed laterally on the buttresses, and the walls, free of the weight, could be nearly all glass. Naturally, this was a stimulus to the art of the stained-glass window, and the sculpture also changed radically to follow the long, vertical lines of the building. (See Plate III.)

Although the Gothic started in France and reached its highest flowering there, it spread all over Europe and in each country was adapted and changed. In southern Europe it became flowing and elaborate, the surfaces enriched with marble and semiprecious stones; in England its character was rigid and mathematical; but in all countries it matured to a certain point and then began to decline. This decline was usually manifested by an overelaboration. The art lost its simplicity and purity until by the fifteenth century the simple, vertical lines that in the twelfth and thirteenth centuries sprang and soared upwards in clean, simple sweeps had become twisted and contorted in what is known as the flamboyant style, from its likeness to writhing flames.

Fortunately, before this art could deteriorate entirely and die out, a new movement began in Italy, the Renaissance.

This was not an outgrowth of the Gothic, but a revolt from it and was due to a rediscovery of the Greek and Roman art of the past. It was such a radical change from the Gothic that it was called a rebirth or *re*-naissance. At this period for the first time the individual artist became important. Hitherto artists had been anonymous, each working in a tradition from which he drew his ideas and to which he contributed, but his own individuality had been felt to be of very little importance—his art was the expression of the art spirit of his race and country, or of the artists of all races and countries. In the Renaissance, however, individual artists signed their works, and their art, while it was, of course, influenced by the whole school or movement, was a highly personal expression of individuality.

It would be well for us to pause a moment and give this period a little more attention than we have been doing in our bird's-eye views of the past, because this art of the Renaissance has conditioned our thinking about art to such an extent that our schools have never yet got free of it. To us art is Renaissance art; it begins and ends there, except for Greek art, which is known to us only by its sculpture and which has become for us a standard for that branch of art. It is true that our artistic roots and traditions (and when I say "our," I mean all European and American art) grow out of the Renaissance. This art appeared suddenly—from Giotto to Leonardo da Vinci was only a matter of fifty years—and it dazzled mankind then and still dazzles us. But we must bear in mind that it was only one expression of the art spirit; there had been many others before, since the dawn of time; there have been many since, and undoubtedly there always will be. The symbols and techniques that the artists of the Renaissance worked out to express their ideas and emotions are only a few out of innumerable possible techniques. Theirs were adapted to their own times and personalities, to their lives and their ways of thought. But three hundred years have passed; new techniques have been developed, new cultures and ways of thought. To hold jealously to a single tradition, native to a people living three hundred years ago in a very small spot in the world, is to limit the possibilities of expression in artists, instead of enlarging them.

It would not be necessary even to state this, except for the fact that the Renaissance art is still held up as a standard in many of our art schools today as though it had been the only art movement of the past and were the only possible tradition for the future. The great movements of the Chinese, Egyptian, and Persian art, as well as many others, are forgotten, and all the exciting discoveries in art in the last three hundred years are ignored. And the last three hundred years have been rich in discoveries and experiments. The Renaissance, however, was the beginning of our conception of realism in art. It introduced perspective and chiaroscuro, two techniques that give a feeling of three-dimensional reality in a canvas. After the static rigidity of the Byzantine these new methods were exciting. We can appreciate and enjoy them, but we must remember that time moves on.

Let us return to our hilltop in the mid-twentieth century and again glance backwards over the historical landscape. We see abrupt slopes and peaks of art rising, now here, now there, all over Europe. Sometimes only an individual artist rises, as El Greco in Spain, or a few men at a time. Sometimes we see a small group of forerunners, then more and more, until a true school emerges, rising to a real movement, as in France, a movement that continues unbroken from the seventeenth century to our own day, gaining in strength all the time. We see the Flemish art emerge, degenerate into illustration, and die out. We see a little flurry in England in the eighteenth

12

century. And all this time, outside the current of European art, mankind everywhere in the world was creating art, because it is man's nature to do so. When a great art movement disappears, art does not entirely die out; it merely falls back to a folk art level, becomes more traditional and less creative.

As we have said before, archeologists constantly are discovering more records of man's art history—in Central and South America, in Africa, in little islands of the Pacific. The record of the past is being enlarged all the time. Exciting discoveries are being made of the art creations of individuals expressing their own inner feelings and the cultures of their times. We see that as long as man has existed art has existed. The production of art, it seems, is a necessary activity of man. Our knowledge of the past gives us the right to conclude that in the future man will continue to create, that movements and schools will rise and fall, that art will change in content and technique, as it reflects men's minds and hearts. The mechanism of those changes will be the same as in the past, first, the differences in individual personalities and, second, the changes in environmental cultures and conditions affecting the artist. We should feel very fortunate that we are living at a point in history where we are heirs to all this richness of the past, and we should welcome the new manifestations of the art spirit when the slow forward movement of time presents them to us.

2

WHAT IS ART?

Now that we have taken this rapid aerial view of thousands of years of man's creative activity, are there any general conclusions we can draw that will help us to a solution of the problem of "What is art"? It appears that this question never troubled men's minds until fairly recently in our history; at any rate, we do not find it in Egyptian papyrus or carved on baked clay tablets. Apparently the people in those days just took art for granted, enjoyed it, and let it go at that. But since man started consciously trying to decide what art is, enough ink has flowed to darken and confuse the whole issue. Here are a few of the definitions that men have painfully forged: Art is beauty. Art is instinct. Art is significant form. Art is expression. Art is communication of feeling. Art is the will to form.

14

Probably all these definitions are true to some extent and all are false to some extent. Some are too inclusive, some too exclusive. "Art is beauty" was for years a favorite and is still backed by a good many aesthetes and art lovers. The catch to that one is obvious. A woman or a rose is beautiful—we all agree on that—but they are not art. And what about African sculpture? Almost everybody feels the power and simplicity of those polished wood and bronze masks and images, but by all our standards of beauty they are ugly. Or, take a Breughel with its hideous imps and monsters. Here we can say that the passages of color are beautiful, but the subject matter is ugly. We see, then, that our standards of beauty are not the same as the standards of beauty held by people a hundred or two hundred years ago or even held by people in different parts of the world today. We look at the paintings of the French or Flemish women of the sixteenth century, with their shaved eyebrows and heads, their bulging eyes, their heavy bodies. They would not have a chance as Miss Atlantic City, 1951. But the painting is still beautiful to us, though the portrayed woman is not. (See Plate IV.) There is a beauty of art and a beauty of nature, and to say that art is beauty does not tell the story. It is too indefinite.

"Art is instinct," too, has its backers, and they put up a good argument for their theory. But instinct is not art, nor is art all instinct; there must be knowledge, too, and under-standing, and a lot more. Instinct alone will not produce great art. There is no doubt that man has an instinct to create; we see it in children and in primitive man and all around us in our daily lives. The creative instinct is strong, and if it is thwarted in its natural channels (not everybody can paint pictures or carve a statue) it bursts forth in all sorts of in-genious ways. The housewife creates a new dish for dinner or hangs curtains that make a subtle color harmony with the

15

wallpaper. The man of the family makes an end table or a miniature locomotive in the workshop in his spare time. So "we put useless buttons on our coatsleeves and parsley round the cold mutton." Of course, a man who is starving to death will not stop to put parsley round the cold mutton, nor will a man dying of cold care whether there are buttons on the coat sleeves. But the very moment the first, most primary needs of man are satisfied, he starts to embellish anything and everything around him with useless ornament. *Useless* in this sense is not derogatory; these embellishments are non-utilitarian, but they have a real use in that they fill that deep dual need in man's nature for creation and enjoyment. If we take stock of the human race, we conclude that the creative urge is instinctive, but to produce a work of art the creative urge must be disciplined and attached to many skills and techniques, and these are not instinctive.

There is much truth, too, in the slogan "Art is significant form." But significant of what and to whom? Significant, obviously, to the spectator, but significant of what raises so many possible answers that it involves us too deeply in speculation and disagreement. For the moment we had better avoid it and try to answer it later, when, we hope, the whole subject has been a little more clarified.

We shall push aside all the definitions of art that have ever been formulated and, starting from the beginning, try to work one out for ourselves. This will be a slow process of building up facts (partly of what art is not), of adding information and example, until we have a kind of shell all round the subject of art, like a hollow mold, into which each reader can pour his own ideas. Perhaps from this will come his own, his perfect definition for himself, personally.

We can safely say that "art is a natural or instinctive activity of mankind," because everywhere that man has existed

16

he has produced art. But when we look at individual examples of these productions, the problem becomes more complicated. It is very hard to see what a carved wood mask produced by an African native in Dahomey has in common with a painting by Holbein produced in Germany in the sixteenth century. Yet we are agreed that both are art. (See Plate V.) Or compare a cave drawing from Altamira in Spain and a Gainsborough or a Renoir. It is difficult to see what all of these things have in common, and yet we must find a common denominator if we are going to discover what art is.

When we compare man's art activity to his other activities, we get another clue. Art is produced as an end in itself; it is not a means to some other end. If primitive man went out hunting, it was to nourish himself and his family. If modern man builds a machine, it is to produce goods that are useful; or if he engages in political activity, it is to the end of bettering the state and man's conditions of living. Everything that man makes with his hands and brain, with the exception of works of art, is made as a means to some other end. But a work of art leads to nothing else; it is important only in itself, and the only result it can have is to arouse an emotion in the spectator. This emotion is self-contained. It does not lead to action. It is valuable only for its effect on the personality of the spectator, not because it influences him to a desired political action or to go out and shoulder a gun and march off to war. Even when art becomes decoration, it is used only for pleasure; the utility of a dish is not increased by embellishing it with designs.

So far, then, we can say that art is an instinctive activity of man and art is an end in itself, leading to nothing, but arousing emotion in the spectator. Obviously this is not a complete definition of art, because the expression of humor, too, is an instinctive activity of man which has no other pur-

17

pose than to arouse an emotion (amusement) in the spectator.

Let us look again at the examples of art that we have chosen to examine and see whether we can discover more principles that they have in common. We see that in painting (and drawing) form is the basic medium of expression—form that is *organized* and that arouses in the spectator an emotion. Now we can look at all the art that has ever been produced at any time or place and see that there have never been exceptions to that rule. All works of art are arrangements of form, organized by the artist in an orderly pattern, and arousing our emotions. In order to arouse our emotions, the artist has had to feel an emotion himself, and his emotion has dictated his arrangement of his forms. A work of art, then, is an expression of the artist's emotion, and the use of forms will differ with each artist because everyone has a different personality, every human being and of course every artist, has something different to express. So although form is the universal medium of artistic expression, the ways of using these forms are infinite, and the emotions they convey are infinite, too. It is possible and useful, however, to classify these types of expression into five categories, provided we bear in mind all the time that all classifications and categories are purely arbitrary and artificial labels and that no exact boundaries can be drawn.

Here are the categories as Frances Blanshard has drawn them up in her book *Retreat from Likeness*. She calls them the stages in the retreat from the conception of painting as likeness to nature toward painting as dispensing entirely with recognizable objects. In other words, painting is classified as more or less abstract, and these stages or degrees correspond to the different types of artist personality, not to different stages in the historical development of art.

18

Type 1. Accurate copy of a particular model.

Type 2. Likeness of the most beautiful parts of many models.

Type 3. Likeness of many models, members of one class (species).

Type 4. Spiritual essence, using the physical object as medium of expression.

Type 5. Complete abandonment of reproduction of natural objects.

These differences in ways of expression, from an exact reproduction of visual nature to complete abstraction which represents nothing in the visible universe, have always existed all through history and correspond to the needs of different types of individuals. They all still exist today. Abstract art, in spite of the hullabaloo raised about its novelty today, has always existed. Although we think of it as something quite new and shocking, a throwing down of all the traditions of art that have been built up during the centuries, we are really thinking only of a very short tradition and a very localized one, the tradition of the Renaissance in Europe. Egyptian, Assyrian, Babylonian, Mayan, and many other arts were highly, though not entirely, abstract.

Let us take up one by one these categories of art as outlined by Blanshard and see whether by analyzing them we can get any farther forward in our search for a definition of art.

Type 1, the photoimage, or exact reproduction of nature, does not appear as an ideal in art until the late Greek period. Before that time, apparently, no one had thought that art was a reproduction or imitation of nature. We know of Greek painting only through the writers of the period—none of the paintings themselves have survived—and we must remember to take the opinions of literary men on painting with a large

19

grain of salt. Then, as now, they had a tendency to apply the rules of their own craft to the art of the painter, but the stories they tell us about the painters and the descriptions of the paintings show definitely that they admired the strictly representational in painting and judged it entirely on realistic grounds. They tell us many a story that proves this point, and these stories have been retold by art critics and teachers in art schools until they have become real old chestnuts.

There is the story of the Greek painter, Parrhasius by name, who painted a picture of cherries that was so realistic that the birds flew into his studio to peck the fruit. This so impressed his rival, Zeuxis, that he invited Parrhasius to his studio to see *his* latest painting. When Parrhasius arrived, he found Zeuxis' picture covered with a curtain, and going up to pull back this curtain, he discovered that it was painted on the canvas.

There are many other stories about the friendly or unfriendly rivalry between these painters, but they are all designed to stress the same point: their ability to reproduce an object on canvas so realistically that it would fool the spectator and even animals. The implication is that this ability is the proper function of the artist, that realism is the quality the artist strives for, and that if we or the birds are tricked into eating the painted cherries, that is the proof of the artist's success.

Plato talks about artists in his dialogues and says that they are not fit for the society of rational men, but his reason is that they are too realistic, they are mere copiers of nature. Compare this with the abuse artists get today because they are not realistic enough!

Can we find any relationship between the degree of realism and the quality of a painting? Is a picture better if it is more like nature? Or is it better the farther it gets away from nature? Looking over the art of the past, we can find good examples of

20

realistic painting and, certainly, many bad examples. A good example is the work of Van der Weyden: in his painting we can see every thread in the cloth, every pore in the skin—and it is great and moving art. (See Plate VI.) Examples of bad photographic realism, without any organization in form, are all around us. This kind of art is on every calendar and magazine cover.

We must conclude that painting can be realistic and good, or realistic and bad, and that "between minute accuracy and aesthetic success or failure, there is no necessary connection." *

In the second category into which we have divided types of art, the likeness of the most beautiful parts of many models, we can again find our examples among the Greek artists. Although their painting is known to us only through the writers, their sculpture has survived, and we can judge it for ourselves. We see that it is not an exact copy of any one model, but an ideal synthesis of many models. The Greeks were a very rational, logical people. They were also humanists; that is, they believed in the value and importance of man. They believed that man himself was the greatest achievement of life, therefore the most beautiful and noblest subject for the artist. It seemed logical to them that definite rules could be worked out for art, as they could for music or mathematics. For example, they applied rules of proportion specific to the human figure. An ideal human being was eight heads high, and every proportion of one part was worked out in relation to every other part. In depicting a woman in sculpture, they modeled the most beautiful head, according to their rules and conceptions, then the most beautiful body, then the most beautiful arms and legs. The completed figure represented finally no one woman, but the composite body of many different women. For a bad example of this type of art we go to the

* Frances Blanshard, *Retreat from Likeness*, King's Crown Press, 1945.

French classicists of the early nineteenth century—for instance, David. The danger of this type of creation is that it becomes intellectual and cold; it loses its emotional content. But here again we see good, as well as bad, examples. In the hands of artists to whose way of thinking this method corresponds, it can be very moving and expressive. Ingres is an example, as is the Roman sculpture, Plate VII.

We see again in Type 3 that both good and bad examples can be cited. Examples of good painting that represent a class, instead of an individual subject, are numerous. Much primitive sculpture represents *man* or *woman* as a class. Japanese painting of a wave or a tree, while it can be very detailed, is obviously *wave* or *tree* in general. (See Plate VIII.) Persian art is largely of this type, and so is much of the painting of our own day. A Braque or Rouault is not a painting of an individual, but a painting of a species, say, *woman* or *clown*. The qualities these artists emphasize are not peculiar to any one woman or clown, but are universal among women and clowns.

Type 4, the painting of the "spiritual essence of things, using an object as the medium of expression," is common to most times and places; there have always been artists who expressed themselves in this way. An artist may express fear by the rushing forms and symbolic shape of a tiger, or religious awe through the use of rising forms and figures which suggest to our minds the mythology of our cults. In this kind of painting the objects or personages depicted are important only to convey a sense of the essential quality they stand for—power in the tiger, wonder and awe in the religious figures. Realism is reduced to a minimum; the emotional content of the form is all-important.

The final division in our gradation from the most to the least realistic types of art is pure abstraction, in which there is no longer a recognizable object. To take examples from the past, we find this abstract art in Scandinavian sculpture, as well as in Celtic, Aztec, and Mayan. (See Plate VIII.) We accept abstract treatment in decoration, in rugs from the Orient, in designs on pottery and textiles, but, because our educators tell us that art should be like the art of the Renaissance and only like that, we have trouble today in accepting abstract art and understanding it. As this seems to be a great stumbling block for most people, we shall go into it more thoroughly in a later chapter, and here only again point out that abstract art can be either good or bad. The degree of abstraction is not related to the quality of the painting.

All the five categories of art we have just glanced over exist because man finds in his nature a necessity for them, because they correspond to different ways of thinking and feeling in different types of man. These types of man have always existed, and therefore these kinds of art, which are a product of man, have always existed, too, simultaneously. Sometimes one type is in the ascendency, sometimes another. It is futile to judge on either a moral or an artistic plane which type is best; you can only say that one type pleases or moves you personally more than another type.

We can see that, besides the long slopes and peaks of art movements which rise out of the plain of the past, we have continuing through history these five types of art, which we might compare to rivers flowing side by side. At different times any one may be wide and deep; at other times it may diminish to a mere trickle; but none of them ever disappears, and every artist working today is the last wave or ripple in one or the other of these five streams. Which channel he follows is determined by his personality structure.

It is plain to us now that the kind of painting—that is, whether it is like life or not—does not determine whether a work of art is good. But wherever we look, in any type of art whatsoever, we find no exception to the rule that form is the medium used by artists to create a work of art. So let us ask ourselves again whether the definition "art is form" is true. We see immediately that it is not; it is much too broad, because it includes all bad art as well as all good art. Bad art, too, uses form as a medium of expression; it is the only thing it has to use. And everything in nature has a form, but forms in nature are obviously not art.

We must be more specific and determine the kind of form that is unique in art. Clive Bell says it is "significant" form. But what does it signify? Does it signify an idea or an emotion which the artist has used it to express? Or may the same work of art signify different things to different spectators? Does not a bad work of art also "signify" something? We may safely answer that a work of art does signify or express the ideas and emotions of the artist, but that a bad work of art does the same.

The same objection can be raised against the definition "art is expression." All art, good and bad, is expression of the artist's ideas and emotions. Our problem is to make our definition more exact, so that it will exclude bad art, yet be broad enough to include all good art.

Let us examine more closely what good artists have done with the forms which we are agreed comprise their medium of expression. They have organized them, unified them. They have taken forms, usually based on or suggested by natural objects, and arranged them in orderly patterns in a limited space. Now, perhaps, we have taken a real step forward in our search for a definition of art. Comparing good art with bad, we find that bad art is usually disorganized; its forms are not arranged in pleasing, harmonious patterns; whereas in a good work of art the arrangements are always organized into some

24

kind of harmonious pattern with an underlying order. Regardless of subject matter, of the degree of representation, whether the picture is realistic or abstract, there must be a systematic organization of the basic forms used.

Perhaps we have now hit on the function of art and the reason that it fulfills a need in mankind. Living in a complex world, so complex that after all these millenniums of man's existence on earth we are only now beginning to grasp a few of the basic facts about the universe around us, we feel confused and lost. One of the great psychological drives in man is to understand his environment. In the most primitive cultures we see man trying to explain the mysterious manifestations of nature, to simplify and organize what he sees around him, so that the mind can grasp it and understand it. Mythmaking is an example of this drive in primitive civilizations, and the work of scientists today is a continuation of the same urge to classify and to organize the natural facts which we observe in our environment into orderly systems. Artists gather from the visual world form and color facts, organizing them into orderly patterns. It is recognized by psychologists, and by almost all the rest of us as well, that pleasure arises from the recognition of clearly organized material. We find rest and relaxation in order; it is a relief from the apparent chaos in which we live.

The facts that the artist chooses from the confused abundance of the visible world and organizes into patterns are not the same kind of facts that the scientist or the novelist chooses. The scientist is like a builder who adds stone on stone to a foundation already laid down for him by preceding workers in his field. He chooses his facts to fit into this foundation, and he chooses them as unemotionally as it is possible for a human being to do. The scientific ideal attitude is strictly impersonal and intellectual. The pleasure we derive from science is an intellectual pleasure, and it goes no deeper than the mind. The artist on the other hand chooses his "facts" on a purely emotional basis. If an object or group of objects moves him, if he reacts with a strong feeling, then these objects become legitimate material for his use. The scientist counts the number of petals in a rose, the size and shape of the various parts. The artist sees the color, the shape of the whole rose, but it is the "fact" of the emotion aroused in himself by the rose that he will try to express through the use of the "rose-facts" of color and shape. He will try to portray not that particular rose, but his feeling for that rose or for roses in general. He must do it through an orderly, easily grasped arrangement of shapes. This means that he must eliminate many things about the rose (or the landscape, or the person) which are there in nature. A choice must be made, and a choice implies that some facts are taken, some are left.

Every simple object in the world is so rich in facts that it is impossible to utilize them all. A chair is, for example, useful to sit on; it has a certain shape and color, weight and size. It changes appearance in different lights; it is comfortable or uncomfortable; it cost a certain amount of money; it is a collection of atoms ceaselessly moving in space. To the cabinetmaker it is obviously hand-turned mahogany; to the owner it has sentimental associations, it is an heirloom from Aunt Julia.

When we look at a landscape, the complications and associations become even richer and more confused. So many natural laws are at work that the effect upon us is one of chaos and disorder. Laws of wind and weather, principles of geology and botany, affect the growth of plants and trees. Seeds are dropped, trees grow, some survive, some are crowded out by others, some are twisted or stunted, some thrive trium-

26

phantly. But the operations of all these laws are not always understood by the mind that perceives the landscape, and nature appears undisciplined and chaotic. The artist chooses from among these confused elements the ones he needs to create a new, orderly, small universe, responding to laws of its own, informed by a unity and simplicity not found in nature.

So far we have determined that art is organized form, that form is the means used by the artist for creating a work of art, and that this form must be ordered and arranged. Now we must ask ourselves whether we can define art as "an orderly arrangement of form." It is clear at once that all orderly arrangements of form are not art. We can think of examples of orderly form which are mere decoration, uninteresting patterns on plates and rugs and pottery. Also, when we were talking about the second of our five artificial categories, we said that some pictures fell into the danger of sterility and lack of emotion through a too careful and calculated organization. Much arrangement of form is banal, dull, and arid. Many paintings intended to be works of art are organized, but the patterns and forms are cold and static, and the mind perceives the order, but the emotions do not respond to it. There are examples in which the order is so apparent and so often repeated that it simply results in boredom in the spectator. Something more, then, is needed before we can call an arrangement of organized form a work of art.

What is this something more? It is the emotional content of the forms employed. The finished product of the artist's labor must express an emotion that he has felt and must convey it to the spectator. It is the quality of this emotion which determines the quality of the work of art.

How are we to determine the quality of an emotion? What distinguishes an "aesthetic" emotion from any other kind of emotion? People who are experienced in the enjoyment of art tell us that there is an aesthetic emotion which is aroused by a work of art and by nothing else, and that this emotion differs from those we feel in our experiences of daily life, in our relationships with people and nature. The difference lies in the fact that the emotion aroused by a work of art is not an incentive to action, nor does it turn us back to ourselves or to our daily lives. This emotion is complete and contained by the work of art itself.

To explain this let us take, for example, a painting of a pretty young girl. If the picture reminds us of a pretty young girl we have known, makes us wish to know this particular pretty young girl, and so on, the picture has not held us. We have been returned to our daily lives, and the emotions aroused are those that would be aroused by meeting a pretty girl in life, but in a weakened degree, because we know that this is not a real pretty girl. The life and personality are missing. So art has done nothing for us that meeting a pretty girl could not do better. The emotions we have felt are emotions designed to lead to action, ultimately to the perpetuation of the race.

Or take another example, a famous old picture which was extremely popular in the art-benighted nineteenth century in England, "The Doctor's Last Visit." This picture arouses emotion; thousands of people have wept over it. If the quantity of emotion aroused is the criterion of the value of a work of art, this picture is surely a masterpiece. It portrays an angelic child dying on a bed, the doctor seated beside her, the sorrowing mother in the background. The emotion aroused is pity, and pity again is a utility emotion; it leads us to go forth and help our fellow man, ameliorate the lot of the poor, the sick and the oppressed.

Before a true work of art we do not want to *do* anything; we simply *feel*. And our feelings are all confined to the object that is arousing them, the work of art. They begin there, they end there, they are completely satisfied. What we are beholding is an end in itself. We are taken out of ourselves and our lives and kept in the new world of the picture, until the experience is over. We are not thrown back on ourselves by references to the world of daily experience in which we live. This world of art is a new world, with its own laws and values which we accept, and the value of our participation in this new world is that we are freed temporarily from our constant need of appraisal and decision on the basis of future action. We do not have to judge or to act; we have only to feel.

This emotional situation is clearer in relation to music. Music has been called the purest of the arts because the medium employed in its creation is not used in daily life. Pure sounds are used only in the composing of music. Poets have to use words which are current coinage for the exchange of ideas and information. They are shopworn from use. Painters use the objects we see constantly before us, smothered in the associated ideas of use. Notes of music alone come to us fresh, not dulled from the usage of our daily lives. Listening to great music, we do not feel pity, shame, love, anger— all those utility emotions designed to goad us to action. We are lifted out of ourselves and our daily lives, we feel that we have had a *new* experience and that it has refreshed and renewed us. We do not ask of music that it represent anything. We know that "The Hunt," in which we can hear the baying of the hounds and the huntsman's horn, is only a trick and a game. We laugh; we do not take it seriously; we know that it is not giving us the emotion that great music should; we are not deceived. In painting, however, we are

29

deceived. We see before us the objects we are accustomed to see in our daily lives; we expect them to be *like* the objects of our daily lives and to arouse the same emotions in us.

The true aesthetic emotion aroused by painting is the same as that aroused by a great work of music. The cause of the emotion is the same: the orderly arrangement of form into a recognizable, harmonious pattern. In music, tones are the medium; in painting, shapes, colors, lines. In music we recognize that the greatness of the music depends on more than the technical ability of the composer, that it depends on the depth and richness of what he has to express, and that his technique is used only as a means to the most complete and perfect expression of his emotion. It is the same in painting.

The subject of any work of art, in any medium, is only the starting point from which the artist departs on the great adventure of creating an entirely new thing. When we listen to a sonata called "Morning," we do not expect to hear reproduced the sounds that are typical of morning in real life. We do not say that the composer has succeeded in his musical composition if he has exactly reproduced the crow of the cock, the rattle of the milk bottles. What we do expect is that he will arouse in us the feeling of freshness, of new beginnings, of renewal, of glory in the rising sun, of the wonder of awakening life. This result is arrived at, not by means of taking bits and pieces of the experience of an actual morning and patching them together, but by *translating* the emotion felt by the artist on all mornings into a new medium, sound. This new medium has its laws and relationships, which are complete in themselves and which give us an added pleasure, the pleasure arising from recognition of order.

When we turn to painting, we become confused by the fact that the materials that the artist uses are the objects we see before us in daily life—not simply abstract tones, but flowers, people, trees—and we shift our standards of judgment. We all know what a tree looks like, and we find ourselves judging a picture on the basis of similarity to reality. "I never saw a tree like that."

If an artist wants to paint a picture entitled "Morning," he may have to use elements from a landscape, perhaps the rising sun, a tree, the horizon. But he uses these concrete objects only as a medium to express the emotion he feels about morning. He embodies his emotion in color, line, and form, and he uses the visual material from the natural world to carry these colors, lines, and forms. In the process of translation from the language of life (a real, growing tree) he freely changes the original object in several different ways. One way is by simplification, another by distortion. Color is keyed up or keyed down; the line is broken, or twisted, or smoothly flowing. It is the artist's right to do this. In fact, it is a necessity for him to do so in order to attain the result that he is seeking, to express his emotion and to arouse emotion in the spectator. When the work of art is completed, the original point of departure in nature, the sunrise or the tree, has become completely irrelevant; it no longer has any connection with the work of art. The picture is a new thing in itself, a new creation which can be judged only by the laws governing works of art, not on the basis of resemblance to the original objects.

You may ask, "Why isn't it sufficient and allowable for an artist to reproduce exactly the scene I see before me in the morning, an exact photographic image of the rising sun, in order to arouse in me the same emotion I feel before nature?"

We have only to remember that the means of creation at the artist's disposal are not the same as the means at the disposal of the Creator of the universe. The artist is working in a small area which is two-dimensional, a limited, flat surface.

31

His colors are pigments, which do not have the range or brilliancy of light. He is restricted entirely to the visual. Therefore he must translate all the material that he uses into the terms of his means.

The emotions we feel before a sunrise are conditioned by the fresh smell of the earth, the coolness of the air, the sound of the crowing cock. All our senses are involved; the sense of distance and space also is a factor in our experience. Then there is the subjective factor, the personal ideas and motives that are bound up with all our thinking and feeling. The farmer sees the sun rising over his fields and knows he must plow them that day; the housewife's enjoyment of the dawn is modified by her realization that the household chores must be done. In a work of art, on the other hand, the artist expresses only the purest emotion of awe at the wonder of the universe, stripped of all mundane considerations and made timeless.

Again we must insist upon a difference in quality in the emotion aroused by a work of art called "Morning" and the emotion aroused by a morning we experience in real life. In a work of art we have the experience of life expressed for us in an orderly, organized form, made understandable to us, made universal, and segregated from all temporary and extraneous considerations. It is not just this particular morning in this particular place, seen by one particular person, but a universal experience common to all men of all times. The amount of this feeling of universality and the quality of the emotion the artist has expressed are the determining factors in the success of a work of art. One might make a rule that the deeper and more universal the emotion expressed by the artist, the greater the work of art.

If this is true, why is there so much controversy over what is good art? Should not anyone be able to feel the artist's emotion immediately, to appraise a work of art at a glance by his own response to it?

We know that there is a great difference of opinion on works of art; some people respond to one type, some to another, and if a picture has the quality of universality, everyone should be able to feel it. The answer is that a work of art is the expression of an individuality and springs out of the • depths of the personality of the artist. There are as many kinds of painting as there are artists producing them. No two persons are alike; no two works of art are alike. Just as we have personal sympathies and antipathies for people based on the needs and responses of our own natures, so we have for pictures. Out of this endless variety of personalities in life and in art, we find and choose what we need, what satisfies and completes us.

Judging art is like judging people. We may recognize that a man is a good man, but we personally cannot love him. But we cannot make laws that would permit only a certain kind of man to exist—say, only men with red hair, or only men who go to the Presbyterian Church—and conclude that only those men are "good" men. Neither can we limit art to the kind of pictures we like. There is and always must be a rich variety in kinds of art; some appeal to me, some to you. Nevertheless, underneath all this variety there lie certain principles which everyone recognizes as good. The form goodness takes in man differs in different societies and at different times. The acts performed by a "good" man in Renaissance Italy would horrify a "good" man in Puritan New England; but reverse their positions, place the Puritan in Renaissance Florence, and he would behave more or less like the Renaissance man. Although the superficial acts and aspects of goodness may differ tremendously, the underlying quality of goodness is there, and it is

33

recognizable underneath the changing external actions which are conditioned by the external factors of time and place.

So it is with works of art. The means of expression, the material way of expressing, change, but underneath all works of art there are qualities and universal principles which are changeless. What these principles are, we will go into in more detail later, but we already know that they are, in general, ordered form, emotion, and universality. Works of art which embody the most universal and the most fundamental facts (psychological or emotional facts) about the world we live in touch us most profoundly and endure the longest.

We have said that the test of a good work of art for you is whether you like it. That and only that is what you can judge it by. The important thing about a work of art for you is your own reaction to it. To revert again to our simile of people, the test of a person for you is whether you like him. But as you mature, your likes and dislikes will change. At twenty you no longer want to associate on an equal level with children of ten. At forty you like still other people. With experience our standards of judgment change. We demand different qualities in our friends. In the same way as we mature in art experience, our demands change with our changing insight and personal development. A great work of art is useless to you if you have not a basis of experience which can respond to the artist's emotion, and because there is such a richness and variety in types of works of art, a variety as great as that of human beings, there will always be works of art to which you cannot respond, whose personality is too different from yours.

The kinds of response of which the spectator is capable correspond to the kind of emotion expressed by different painters. We have classified types of painting into five artificial categories, roughly corresponding to degrees of realism and

34

abstraction. The more realistic types of painting will please people who are visual-minded, who receive their strongest sensations through the sense of sight. Then there are people who will always value painting as a substitute for something in life, as a souvenir of a pleasant experience, which recalls it on demand. There are people who will appreciate classes 2 and 3 of our categories, the likeness of the most beautiful parts of many models, or the likeness of a synthesis of many models— members of one class or species. These are the people who appreciate order above emotion, who are logical idealists, who want the good, but want it ordered by strict rule. They are able to think in abstract generalities, but only to a certain extent. They are like the scientists who can recognize and classify an example of a species, but cannot relate it to a larger organization, to other species, and to the underlying truths and generalities. There are people who can go a step farther into generalized thinking and who will respond to category 4, in which the physical object portrayed is a symbol of the spiritual essence of the class of objects (as strength or ferocity represented by a tiger). And, finally, there are people who are accustomed to thinking in large abstract terms and who will recognize and be moved by the abstract, underlying principles in a purely nonrepresentational art.

No one can say that one type of good person is better or worse than another, and so no one can say that one type of good painting is better or worse than another. We can only say that a painting accomplishes its purpose more or less fully. The purpose of art is to move us, to arouse emotion in us. A good work of art can be truly judged only by time. If it moves a great many people over a long period of time, we agree that it is good. Most people with art experience or training agree, on the whole, about what is and what is not good art. They may and do respond more fully to some kinds than to others, but they do agree, on the whole, particularly about pictures that are removed from us by time. We can more easily be fooled and confused by pictures painted today. Our choice is wider and we must distinguish between much bad art that time will eliminate and some good art whose quality may be disguised for us by novelty or obscured by the prejudices of fashion. While waiting for time to help us in our decision, the only safe rule to follow is that art for us is what we like. If we like pictures that the knowledgeable and discriminating say are not art, it is probably that we have not yet matured in our art lives, and time and experience will correct that lack. Or it could be that the discriminating person is wrong. No one is infallible.

In the world of good art there is something for everyone, for every type of person from the most literal to the visionary.

Now let us go back once more and see what progress we have made toward a definition of what art is. We have seen that the basis of art is form, that this form must be organized, and that organization of form alone is not enough; it must express an emotion felt by the artist and that emotion must be imparted to the spectator. We have also concluded that the quality of a work of art depends on the quality of the emotion expressed, that if the emotion is universal in scope and can be felt by most men, regardless of time or place, the work of art may be said to be great. Works of art with a more limited appeal, whose content of emotion can be felt only by a more or less circumscribed group of men of a certain country or period, are lesser works of art, valid though they may be on a temporary basis. We have also seen that resemblance to the model or object in nature is completely irrelevant in our judgment of a work of art. A picture is a newly created thing, quite independent of the original object

36

Cave drawing done so long ago that no one can estimate its age within a few thousand years. (Frobenius Collection, Frankfurt am Main.)

T'ang Horseman   PLATE I

Han Figurines

We sense that the sculptors who produced these figures thought and felt very much as we think and feel today. (Courtesy of the Metropolitan Museum of Art.)

Reproduction of a
Ravenna Mosaic

The simplification of
shapes and the modeling
of flattened planes endears
the art of the Byzantines
to the modern artist.
(Courtesy of the Metro-
politan Museum of Art.)

PLATE II

"Head of Christ" by Rouault

Rouault is much closer in temperament to a Byzantine artist
than he is to any of his contemporaries. (Private collection.
Photo, courtesy of The Museum
of Modern Art, New York.)

Stained-glass Window, Chartres Cathedral

The impetus given to art in the twelfth century was the advance made in architecture. This made possible the stained-glass window. The sculpture also changed radically to follow the vertical lines of the buildings.

PLATE III

A Memling Madonna

A woman considered beautiful in Memling's time is not our ideal of a beautiful woman today. Standards of beauty change from country to country and from period to period. (St. John's Hospital, Bruges.)

PLATE IV

African Head

We must find a definition of art that will not exclude this simplified wood carving from Gabun. (Madame Helena Rubinstein Collection. Photo, courtesy of The Museum of Modern Art, New York.)

PLATE V

ANNO.1532.   ÆTATIS SVÆ.29.

Portrait of a Member of the Wedigh Family by Holbein

Nor this realistic portrait by Holbein. Both succeed in being works of art in spite of the vastly different cultures and points of view they reflect. (Courtesy of the Metropolitan Museum of Art.)

"Annunciation" by Van der Weyden

A good example of photographic realism. We see every detail, every thread and every hair, and it is great and moving art. (Courtesy of the Metropolitan Museum of Art.)

PLATE VI

PLATE VII   Roman Copy of a Fifth-century Greek Sculpture

An example of "ideal" art. It represents a composite of the most beautiful parts of many models selected on the basis of an ideal standard.   (Courtesy of the Metropolitan Museum of Art.)

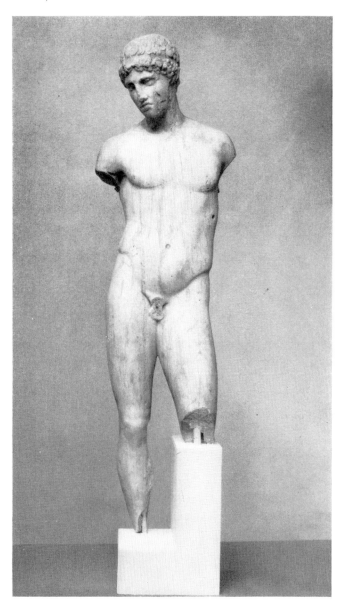

Temple of the Two Lintels, Chichen Itza, Yucatan

In the sculpture as well as the manuscripts of the Mayans we find a highly abstract art.

Plate VIII

Japanese Painting by Hiroshige

Japanese painting does not represent a particular wave or tree but the idea of *wave* or *tree* in general. (Courtesy of the Metropolitan Museum of Art.)

which started the creative process, and not to be judged by the same standards. In a hundred years no one will care whether the portrait resembled Aunt Nellie; the spectator will care only whether the forms and colors the artist used moves him, whether the artist has succeeded in giving him a new and rich experience. If the artist has not done this, if the portrait is simply a reproduction of Aunt Nellie with her personal characteristics—item, brown eyes; item, gray hair; item, mole on left cheek—the picture will be classified among family souvenirs of interest only to Aunt Nellie's descendants or will have found its way to attic or junk shop. In Holbein's paintings of people, in some of Renoir's, in many of Manet's and Gauguin's, we feel the individual character but also the universal character. In all great pictures that endure there is found the universal quality, although there may be present also the characteristics of one individual. The spectator recognizes the "Aunt Nellyness" of all Aunt Nellies, or some quality of universal application.

It is apparent by now that there are three elements involved in a work of art: first, the artist; second, the product of the artist's brain, or the work of art; third, the spectator. All three are essential. The first two are obviously so, but a work of art without a spectator is inconceivable; it is a work of art only *because* of its effect upon a spectator. The more discriminating spectators there are, the more good art will the artist produce; an understanding demand for good art makes a favorable soil in which art can grow. Therefore it is important for us to decide what we demand in art.

Now we should be able to ask ourselves again the question "What is art?" We find that even now we have arrived at no hard and fast definition of art itself, but we have been able to come to certain conclusions as to what art should do for us:

37

It must, through the use of form, organize visual and perceptual material into orderly arrangements, thus clarifying and bringing light to bear on ourselves and the world in which we live. Once we have determined the function of a thing, we are a step nearer to an understanding of the thing in itself, and we have now a working basis to build on, a foundation for a further analysis of works of art.

3

WHO IS THE ARTIST?

A t one time there was a picture in the popular mind of a pale, long-haired, long-fingered, dreamy-eyed, creature seated in a high ivory tower. This was "The Artist." This picture was gradually transformed into one of a violent, velvet-coated, bearded savage, living in an attic, feeding on bread crusts and red wine, and given to outbursts of temperament, such as the slashing of his canvases with palette knives. In both these mental pictures the artist was set apart from the rest of humanity by his appearance and character. He was an oddity, partly laughable, partly frightening. You never knew what he might do. This impression of the artist still lingers in the back of some people's minds, but for the most part we now think of the artist simply as a man who looks more or less like a human being and who creates works of art. There should be no problem for us, then, in determining who is the artist. He is anyone who creates a work of art.

When we look around us, we see thousands upon thousands of people making images on paper, on canvas, on any surface available. Miles of walls are covered with tons of paint; millions of greeting cards, postcards, illustrations, magazine covers, calendars are turned out every day. Designs in black and white, in color, on dishes, on fabrics, on objects of use and of no use are created by someone or thousands of someones. Are all these someones artists?

We see that again it is essential to determine which of these millions of images that are flooding the world are art and which are not. Upon that hinges the question of who is the artist. It is not necessarily the man who puts paint on canvas, as distinguished from the man who draws on paper, nor is the criterion to be found in the fact that one so-called work of art is framed and hanging in a museum and the other is printed in the daily paper and thrown away after a glance. Some very great artists have made drawings for what was then analogous to the daily paper; Daumier and Hogarth are two examples. But we know now that art is a matter neither of technique nor of materials. We know, at least roughly, what a work of art is, or at any rate we have an area of knowledge which contains works of art of which we are sure, surrounded by a larger area of works of art of which we are doubtful. This field of understanding and appreciation of specific works of art is changing and always will be as long as we are growing and developing. Some types of works of art will move out of the surrounding indeterminate areas of our understanding into the sure area; others of which we now feel sure will take a secondary place. Even the most expert of art lovers have these boundaries separating the art of which they are sure from the equivocal art.

What about these images with which our eyes are bombarded daily, in magazines, papers, books, on billboards, on walls? The men who create these images are working in the field of art; they are using the medium of the artist, and many of these productions can and do give us pleasure. They tell us a story, give us information, remind us of past pleasurable experiences, and now and again give us the thrill of a real aesthetic experience, because amid this mass of material we do find the work of a real artist. Even that old symbol of bad art, the calendar, can be a good work of art—look at the Pepsi-Cola calendar. It pays to keep your eyes open, as well as your mind, every time you look at a magazine or a poster; sometimes you find a treasure. Of course, most of the ephemeral productions in the art medium that we meet in our daily lives are not art and have no pretension of being so. The men who produce them have a necessary part in our lives; we need them, too; but they are not the creatures we are tracking down. Our game is the real creative artist, and we will try to segregate him and can examine him at our leisure.

We have repeated again and again that the creative urge in mankind is instinctive and strong. It is one of our underlying driving forces. If it is blocked in one way, it finds an outlet in another way. Even in the limited sense in which we are using the word "artist," that is, confining it to those who have produced a nonutilitarian work in the creative area we have discussed, and eliminating the creative housewife and her flowers or the creative man of the house and his workshop— even in this limited meaning we find that almost without exception everyone has produced works of art in his lifetime. All normal children pass through a creative period during which

41

they often create works of art that are valid by any standards. It is only because we have built up false conceptions of art that we do not recognize the value of these childish productions. We are accustomed to seek art in museums only, to recognize it only when it is set apart and labeled "Art," instead of reacting to it wherever it is found. Also we confuse art and technique. The directness and simplicity of a child's drawing makes us take for granted its inadequacy, but we often find in children's drawings everything which we have the right to demand from a work of art—a direct expression of an emotion or attitude toward life expressed with the most economical means. What we do not find is the depth and power of a mature artist.

There is much to be gained in understanding of the nature and development of art from the proceedings of children, and many psychologists and artists have studied and are studying this question. They have discovered that children all over the world, of any language or nation, develop along identical paths in creative growth. There are innate ways of art expression, and in a logical and orderly sequence these ways unfold and lead to the next step. Every child in the world goes through these stages of development, regardless of training or any other outside influence.

Here are the stages of development that all of us have passed through as children: First, the scribbling stage, which explains itself. The child is interested simply in the fact that the object he holds makes a mark on the paper. His coordination of hand is not sufficient to control these marks, and he has not yet made the connection between representation and the marks on the paper. At first the child scribbles with his whole arm controlled by shoulder and elbow, a swinging scribble with broad, simple strokes. Gradually these strokes become more differentiated and shorter and more numerous. Forms

42

are made at first in almost straight lines and without interruptions, then by circular lines, and finally in spirals. Next comes the later scribbling stage. The child, more or less accidentally, makes a form which suggests to him an object. He elaborates on this form to bring it closer to the object it has suggested. The next stage reached by the child is the preschematic stage. This stage is characterized by a constant search for a method of representing form. It has no fixed aspect. We see at this stage the greatest variety of form symbols representing the same object. The child gradually creates his own expressive symbols for every form. This is a turning point in his development. Schematic drawing begins to predominate. The next phase is the schema stage. By *schema* is meant a definite symbol evolved to stand invariably for each object to be represented. A circle for a head is a simple example, or dots with a curve above for eyes. At this stage no further changes in form are created by the child to represent reality. Symbols are crystallized personal characteristics represented in schema form. Some of the symbols may be tactile (representing the touch feeling of objects); some are connected with the muscular feelings linked to the rhythmical scribbling which preceded this stage.

The child at first names his pictures only after they are complete, but with increasing practice, he gives names to them while he is drawing and, finally, before beginning to draw.

We have said that symbols are crystallized personal characteristics. We see that even in the earliest stages of drawing art creation is an expression of the individuality, even though all children pass through the same stages of development. What they have to express and how they express it remains a personal matter. The schema developed by the child has its roots in his personality total. The very earliest schema is bound

43

up with the individual self. Even the personal characteristics of the child are represented. For instance, a crippled child draws human beings misformed on the same side he is. The anxiety of another child may be represented by uncertain, quavering lines. These facts are important to note; the natural basis of art is in the deep, unconscious personality, the instinct, of the artist. Consciously or unconsciously he will reveal himself through his work. "All artistic ability has its roots in universal human dispositions. It is determined only by the exceptional intensification of the abilities of certain individual senses." *

When the child has arrived at the schema stage of drawing he is satisfied, he has worked out a way of expression that says everything he wants to say. The connection with visual reality may be slight. The child is not trying to draw things as they look but as he feels them. This is another thing that cannot be emphasized too strongly if one really wants to understand art. From the first appearance of the art impulse the representation of seen objects is not the drive in artistic creation. What the child is trying to portray is what he knows or feels about the things around him. Even after a child has very good muscular control and can count, he may continue to draw a hand that is a circle completely surrounded by fingers. He may know that a hand has only five fingers, but he feels the importance of fingers for grasping and touching, and this feeling is interpreted by an exaggeration of the number of fingers on the hand. Children's art is "abstract" or nonrealistic, not from lack of ability to reproduce nature as it is (this is true certainly in the later stages) but because the fundamental urge in art is for self-expression. The child sees no reason to reproduce what is already before him, but has a strong desire to express himself. Lowenfeld says, "We may assume

* O. Wulff, *Die Kunst des Kindes.*

44

that neither the development nor the formal aspects of the human schema (the child's symbols to represent human beings) have anything whatever to do with the experiences of the sense of sight." These are strong and positive words, but other workers in child study bear them out. The child is trying to express what he knows, not what he sees. The order he arrives at in his picture is an order of knowledge, and in that knowledge are included all the sensory experiences that promote or impinge upon it—touch, taste, muscle feeling, etc. (See Plate IX.)

The forms that the child achieves are a synthesis of all these different sensory experiences. Up to the ninth year muscular experiences play a large part in child drawing. The part of the picture that is most strongly felt by the body is elaborated in detail and exaggerated in size. A man lifting has long arms; a man grasping has elaborated hands. This is the way we feel these things in the muscles when we are lifting and grasping. Muscular effort is felt in clenching our teeth; in a drawing of a person making such an effort the teeth will be important, because the body feels them so. The spectator, too, should feel the effort in his nerves and muscles. Sensations in the body itself are a child's first experiences and play such an important part in his drawing that some psychologists have thought that this bodily feeling is the underlying principle of drawing.

Even in adult art a larger part is played by bodily sensations than we realize. Our muscular reaction takes place unconsciously; when we see an object which looks heavy, all our muscles react as though to prepare us to lift. This bodily feeling is called *kinesthetic*, and the people who feel things primarily in this way, whose strongest reactions to surrounding stimuli are felt in the body itself, have been labeled *haptic*. This is a short and convenient word, and we shall use it to

45

distinguish this type of personal reaction to life from the reaction primarily to sensations through the eyes, which is characteristic of the *visual* type of person.

The game of naming things is lots of fun, but we must remember that it is only a game, or at the best it provides a rough simplification of the underlying realities that the names stand for and makes facts easier for us to handle. Classifications do not exist in nature; they appear only in our man-made game. Some scientists and some art critics lose sight of this truth and spend their whole lives playing the naming game without a thought for the reality that the names stand for. When we divide mankind into haptic and visual types, we are playing the game of names. In reality there is no hard and fast division; there is only a matter of degree. No one is purely visual or purely haptic. In all adults these reactions are mixed, but when one or the other predominates, we shall use the label for convenience.

Children are more strongly haptic than adults, but as we look carefully at examples of works of art by great adult painters, we are conscious that in many the artist has felt very strongly in his own body the strain of muscles, the weight of objects, and communicated this sensation to us. Works of art can be easily divided on analysis into those most strongly felt by the body and those which appeal principally to the eye. In the former the artist himself has felt and expressed the bodily sensations by means of visual symbols; in the latter the artist has expressed an emotion which takes place in the mind and has been aroused by the visual aspect of things, by the way things look.

Kinesthetic, or bodily, sensations have been understood as a legitimate basis of art, and symbols to express these sensations have been consciously evolved by modern artists. Some of these symbols have been found in child art and in primitive

46

art and adapted to the use of the modern artist. Our epoch has been one of great research and experimentation in art. Attempts have been and are being made to explore all the means of artistic expression, and the symbols used by children, which are also used in a very similar way by primitive peoples, have shown that there are natural, instinctive ways of expressing emotion through forms.

Thus we may say that all children are artists. They express themselves naturally, instinctively, in drawing and in surprisingly similar ways. The children of Japan, of Central Africa, of Europe, of America, pass through the same stages of artistic evolution. The basis of their art is not visual; it is an expression of what the child feels and knows about the world, not of what he sees. Long after he can measure and count, he may continue to draw a head twice as large as the body or fringes of innumerable fingers on the hand if he feels the importance of heads or fingers in what he is trying to say in his picture. Anyone who has worked with children knows how sure they are when they are drawing. They know exactly what they want to do. Until very late in childhood they have no self-doubt or doubt of their ability to put on paper what they wish to express. Of course, some children are more talented than others. They pass through the stages of development more quickly; they have a richer and more original vocabulary than the average. But all children with all degrees of talent pass through the stages listed above. No steps are ever skipped in the chain of development, and all children finally arrive at a self-conscious stage at which visual reality becomes stronger than their inner sensations and a conflict is set up.

This is the point at which most of us cease forever to be artists and unfortunately also cease forever to be interested in art. We want to conform, we want to be accepted, and the

47

opinions and value judgments of those around us become important to us. On all hands we hear that a picture must "look like" the subject. Exact reproduction of the visual, surface appearance of things is held up to us as the aim of art. "Mary's mouth is not that big." "Her nose is shorter." And so we lose interest because subconsciously we do not care a pin whether Mary's mouth is big or small. That detail is vastly unimportant, and therefore art becomes unimportant, too. We decide to leave it to the "artist," not realizing that perhaps we are "the artist," that perhaps what we were trying unconsciously to express about Mary's mouth was more true than the dimension in fractions of an inch. This training in looking for unimportant visual facts goes on until even our pleasure in looking at pictures is spoiled; our parents and teachers, our books on art tell us that one thing is important —factual fidelity, imitation of visible nature—while our instincts tell us another, that the important thing is the feeling imparted. Eventually our feelings are stifled, are buried out of sight, and atrophy from lack of use. Our lives begin to be filled with other interests, with our social instincts and adjustments. The life of the spirit is starved and we do not even realize our spiritual hunger any more.

This is what happens to you and me, but what happens at this point to "the artist"? In school there were perhaps two or three children in the class who had a particular aptitude for art. Let us call these three children Johnny, Jimmy, and Jane.

Let us say that Johnny's father is an artist of the realistic school, mediocre but successful as a painter of photographic portraits. He receives the news from his son's teacher that Johnny is a talented boy. He is pleased. His son will follow in his footsteps; he, too, will paint society women and heads of colleges and oil companies and make a good living doing it.

48

Johnny has no doubt that painting portraits that look like photographs is art and that his father is an artist. (Why should he doubt? His father is head of important art societies; he makes lots of money; he gives talks to women's clubs.) Still Johnny has seen the seamy side of the life of this kind of artist. He knows that his father is less free than the most menial servant, that his life is spent in using his technical ability to flatter the egos of "important" people who want posterity to think of them as handsome, imposing, and superb. Johnny decides to be an auto mechanic.

Now Jimmy's father is an auto mechanic. It troubles him when Jimmy's teachers send a note home recommending that Jimmy be sent to an art school for special training. Jimmy's father knows that artists are eccentric guys who lead a loose life and never make a dime. He feels his responsibility as a father, and he loves his son. He does not want him to make a mistake now that would spoil his life forever. The father is an adult; the son is only fourteen years old. How can the boy know what is best for himself? So the father decides for Jimmy, and though Jimmy rebels at first, he finally submits and becomes an auto salesman and marries. Sometimes he tells his wife what a foolish ambition he had when he was a boy. He wanted to be an artist! But sometimes, when they are on their vacation at the seashore and he is watching the waves beating on the shore, or sometimes when he glances up from his order book and sees the blue sky with streaks of fantastic white cloud, he has strange stirrings of feeling within him that something is lacking in his full life.

And now we come to Jane. Jane, too, has teachers who find that she is talented, and she has parents who have her welfare at heart. They are good parents and, of course, they want Jane to marry a man of their own social position who can support her. They want her to have children, a nice home, and

49

security, and they consider that Jane is more likely to meet the right type of man in college than in art school. But as Jane's heart seems to be set on going to art school, they reluctantly consent. Jane goes off to art school, where she carries off all the prizes, but where she also meets a young art student with whom she falls in love. She wants to marry this art student, and he wants to marry Jane, but in order to marry the young art student has to have a job so that he can support a wife. So he gets a job in an advertising firm drawing women's fashions, and Jane becomes a good wife and mother and never draws again except to amuse her children on a rainy afternoon.

There you have the imaginary but very probable story of the three most talented children in an art class. But, you say, none of them became an artist. Who, then, does become an artist? It is very likely that from this particular art class no one became an artist. The statistics are not available but certainly not more than one person in several thousand follows art as a career. Let us continue our imagining and see what happens to the three next most talented children, Freddy, Frank, and Fanny.

Freddy is a dreamy boy who is not good at baseball nor very good at arithmetic. He has an older brother who is very good at both these things and is very popular, besides. Freddy's parents are always comparing Freddy with his brother, much to the disadvantage of the former. But Freddy can draw, and his brother cannot, and the ability to draw, while it does not give him as much prestige as the ability to play baseball, is Freddy's only social asset. It is the only thing for which he receives praise, and so, even after the other children have stopped expressing themselves in drawing, Freddy continues to make pictures and to find an outlet in this way for his feelings of isolation and rejection. When he reaches adolescence, his family allow him to go to art school because he is dreamy and impractical and will never make a successful businessman.

For these negative reasons Freddy is launched on his career as an artist. In art school Freddy is taught a great many things about how to make a photographic likeness of the model and about the techniques used by artists in the Renaissance; or if Freddy lives in one of the larger cities in the United States and attends a modern progressive art school, he learns how to paint an abstract picture by formula. But Freddy looks about him at all the works of art that he can find in books and in museums, and he sees that a great deal that he is being taught does not apply to many of the works of art that he admires. He accepts some and rejects some of the teaching of the school, and the rest of his life is spent in a satisfying search for a true and personal way of expressing his own feelings. He becomes a real artist.

Let us say that Frank, too, becomes an artist, that his background of family and environment is different, and that therefore the circumstances determining his choice of a career are different. There are as many reasons for the choice of art as a career as there are people and circumstances, but let us say that Frank's family is very poor and that the objections to his studying art are purely financial. But Frank can study art on the G.I. Bill—or, if Frank was born a few years earlier, on the P.W.A. art project—and as there are few jobs available, Frank might as well be doing that as anything else while he is waiting for a job to turn up.

Frank finds very soon that he has a great facility and skill, that he has a knack of assimilating techniques and styles. He works out a fresh, appealing technique which is a combination of the styles of several popular artists of the day. His work has charm, and an art dealer signs him up on a contract. His work sells. He makes a quick success because his pictures are easily understood; they are like other pictures that the public has seen, and still they have a certain freshness which superficially can be confused with originality. So Frank makes quite a lot of money and goes on painting the same picture on different canvases for years, until he can turn out a painting by formula with his eyes shut. Of course he gets very bored at times and tries to paint a new picture, or to experiment and branch out, but when he does this, his art dealer and the critics and his public all set up a clamor and threaten his livelihood by refusing to buy his new work. Then he goes back to the same old thing again, until finally he is covered with honors and medals, his students look upon him with awe and respect, he is the grand old man of American painting, and he even looks upon himself with awe and respect and tries to keep down all the younger painters who do not paint in exactly the same way he does.

One more imaginary story of a child who became an artist, and we are ready to draw some generalized conclusions as to who the artist is and why he chooses this career. Let us see what happens to Fanny. Fanny's father belongs to the educated class; he is a lawyer and a cultivated man. He even has hanging in his living room some real, hand-painted oil paintings which he inherited from a distant relative. He has an Inness and a Blakelock, and he knows that they are extremely valuable, because his relative paid a lot of money for them a good many years ago. Fanny's father knows that they are "Art" and that the highest form of "Art" is misty landscapes with a lot of thick paint and varnish on them, and he is quite unaware of any pictures painted later than "The Blue Boy." He is rather pleased when Fanny wants to be an artist and sends her to the best private art school in their town. By one of those miracles which occur now and then, there happens to be at this art school a very good teacher, who realizes that an artist is not made by forcing him into a mold of rules and techniques, but that in every human being there lies the seed of the artist and that the teacher's job is to prepare a favorable soil in which this seed can grow and develop in its own way.

After a few years of hard work, Fanny starts bringing home canvases which are original, which display a new point of view and a personal technique. But her father and all her circle of friends know that this is not "Art." Where are the misty landscapes and the rich, pasty masses of paint and the charm and poetry of the "The Blue Boy"? A conflict is set up in Fanny, because she respects her father and his friends, and she was brought up to revere the Blakelocks and the Inneses.

When she marries, as such girls invariably do, her husband, too, admires the misty landscapes, but he is very kind and indulgent about her own painting and assures her that in time she, too, will be able to paint good pictures worthy of a gold frame. But for the next ten years Fanny has no time to paint. She is taking care of the children and entertaining her husband's business associates. Now and then she remembers that she is an artist, and she makes drawings of her babies, drawings which are very good resemblances, because the important thing to Fanny is how her children look. She wants to remember, when the children are grown, how they looked when they were small. When Fanny finally has a little leisure after her children are away at school, she buys a paintbox and says, "Now, at last, I can be an artist." Her friends and acquaintances bring their children to Fanny to have their portraits painted, because Fanny has a knack of catching a likeness. This is easy for her and pleases everybody. This facility brings her money and prestige, and by this time the influence of her art-school teacher has grown dim. Her father and friends were right, and the art-school teacher was a "long-hair," a term of contempt in her circle. The end of this story is that Fanny, like Frank, becomes a very noted artist and an influence and model for all the young artists in her town.

What do the stories of these six artists signify? Perhaps they show that one out of six painters, making a living (or trying to) by their art, is a real artist and that is a generous estimate. It shows, too, that the career of an artist is full of pitfalls, a few of which are the pressures brought to bear upon him by his dealer, by his friends and family, by his economic responsibilities; that the rewards are great in our country for the artist who has technical skill and a facility for making photographic likenesses. These are some of the external pitfalls, but the inner struggles, doubts, and difficulties in the process of assimilating the art influences of the past and forging a perfect implement for self-expression are greater still. The miracle is that anyone ever manages to be a real, great artist. Art in most of the environments in the United States is belittled and undervalued. "You can't make a living at it" is the attitude of parents when a boy wants to be an artist, and toward a girl there is usually a condescending attitude that she is pursuing a dilettante avocation which cannot be taken seriously, or that she is simply marking time till she is married. It takes a very strong creative urge for anyone to come to a determination to be an artist and to continue in that career.

Dr. Anne Roe has been doing some valuable work on this subject and has published several papers on it in technical journals. She made a thorough study of the lives and work of twenty of our best-known and most successful artists and drew some extremely interesting conclusions. She compares the reasons that people become artists with the reasons that people enter other professions and tries to define the artist's

54

personality as distinct from the personalities of other professionals.

She says that there are two drives in human beings: A drive toward a mastery of the environment, "to impose his intrinsic determination upon a widening realm of events," is known as the drive toward *autonomy*. The second drive or urge in human nature is toward *homonomy*, and this "expresses the tendency of human beings to share and to participate in, to fit into and to conform with, superindividual (or outside the self) categories such as the family, the social group, a meaningful world order, etc. Characteristic examples of the trend toward homonomy are social, religious, ethical, and aesthetic attitudes." It was found that in nearly all artists this latter trend, the trend to lose oneself in something external and larger than oneself, was very strong. Here we have immediately a contradiction of the old idea of the artist as an egocentric individualist, submerged in his work and living an antisocial life apart.

But what we are most interested in is what Dr. Roe found out about the type of men who become artists and why they choose that profession. Here is how she summarizes her findings:

> Choice of this vocation, so far as I was able to learn, did not result solely from special abilities, nor primarily from a particular personality pattern, nor from any disparate [separate] elements in the personality so far as we are now able to isolate them. Study of the individual lives, however, makes it clear that this profession does satisfy emotional needs for most of the men which have not been satisfied in other ways, and gives us a clue not only to the meaning of creativeness, but to the meaning of all work activity.

55

In other words, no one type of personality becomes an artist; these artists had only one thing in common, that they were getting a satisfaction out of their work, and if this were not the case, they undoubtedly would not have continued in it.

Let us give another quotation from Dr. Roe which again accents the fact that all kinds of people become artists. Dr. Roe says, "The artists showed extreme heterogeneity [differences] in the general personality structure presented, and to my astonishment, many of them did not give any of what we have supposed to be indications of creative ability. Though some tendencies appeared in most of the group, these did not distinguish them from all other groups" (that is, groups of other professions). After saying again that half the group gave no striking indications of creative ability and that in some of these men the indications were quite to the contrary, Dr. Roe continues, "Yet these men are demonstrably artists, and successful ones at that." She concludes that either the tests always used to indicate creative ability are at fault or that "one may be a successful artist in our society without having creative ability." Personally, I am inclined to fear that the latter is the case.

Dr. Roe's study of the lives and backgrounds of these men show that their reasons for becoming artists are as various as their personalities. They have only the one thing in common, that all were finding in their work an emotional satisfaction, but even this differs in that art satisfied different emotional needs in each individual. In glancing over the brief abstracts of the lives of these twenty painters, the eye is struck by another thing they have in common which is not mentioned by Dr. Roe. All of them had unhappy childhoods, in the home, or from racial persecution in school, or because of the loss of a parent at an early age. Dr. Roe draws no conclusions from this, but could it be one of the determining factors in the choice of art as a profession? Many people who have had unhappy childhoods do not become artists, but we remember that all these men were of the homonomous type, men who had a trend toward losing themselves in a larger whole, toward the absorption of their personality into something outside themselves. Art is one kind of larger whole, outside the individual. One becomes a member of a large and timeless group, a link in a long chain of others of one's kind. Again it is necessary to point out that many people have this urge to lose themselves in something outside themselves, something larger than they are, and do not become artists. They join the church or the Elks' Club.

Chance seems to play a large part in determining who becomes an artist. Many of the most talented art students drop out under the pressures of our economic civilization, which places such handicaps in the way of the artist and offers such brilliant rewards in other fields. Many of the least talented continue and even make a success financially in art, if they happen to have the qualities which would have made a financial success in any other field they had entered. The only conclusion we can draw is that there is no artist type, no strange, egotistic personality set apart from his fellow men from the beginning and carrying the mark of genius on his brow. There are only men like you and me, who happened for one reason or another to become artists instead of doctors or mechanics and most of whom, if they followed their profession sincerely, found in it greater psychological rewards and greater adventures of the spirit than are found in most other fields. Nearly all of us have the feeling that we could have been artists if the circumstances had been right, and the strange thing is that it is true.

Too much stress should not be placed, however, on the part

57

that is played by chance in the choice of art as a profession. It is true that chance plays the same part in that choice as it does in the choice of other careers. Very few of us are born with a very strong bent toward being a doctor or a farmer; only the fortunate few are sure at an early age of what they want to do with their lives. Most of us have capacities for many things; we have possibilities that could have been developed; we might have led many lives. Once a profession is chosen, determined perhaps by our families, our environment, or our own talents and capabilities, it is certain that unless we get enough satisfactions from our jobs, we will not continue in them.

This is particularly true of art as a career, for, contrary to common belief, art entails a tremendous amount of hard physical work. This work is done alone, not in company with one's fellows, where pleasant social contacts may furnish the pleasure that is lacking in the job itself. Also, the rewards of financial gain and prestige are long delayed in the artist's career. Only in very exceptional cases does an artist become well known before reaching middle age. It takes years for an artist to overcome the technical difficulties inherent in the task of expressing an emotion in terms of color, line, and form. And besides the difficulties of the medium itself, the translation of something as fleeting and as abstract as an emotion into a language of concrete forms, the artist must grow and ripen emotionally so that he has deep experiences to express. All of this takes time and work, and meanwhile he is usually suffering from a lack of understanding and appreciation, as well as a lack of money. It is obvious that he must find his rewards in the work itself, and it is not a matter of surprise that many artists who have the possibility of producing great and good art, if given time, fall by the wayside and either leave art altogether or paint what the art dealers

58

and the public will buy. The artist must be single-minded; he must paint out of himself and for himself. Only in that way can he truly paint for others. The moment he paints what he thinks others want, or even what they do really want, or paints for money, a dual point of view is set up, and the necessary singleness and unity that produce a true work of art are lost.

Our conclusion is that we all start out as potential artists, though some of us have a better equipment of the necessary qualities of sensibility, visual perceptiveness, technical facility, etc., than others; but outside factors determine in most cases the choice of art as a career, and this choice is often based on other factors than capability. Some of the best potential artists never become artists. In our society art is penalized. Only one in several thousands of good, or at least honest, artists can exist financially by painting alone. Artists must teach or otherwise make a living by some means outside their art. Society is piling up a debt toward the artist who is carrying out his necessary function in the face of great obstacles and often personal suffering. According to the public and the critics, the personal rewards and satisfactions of being a painter are so great that they should suffice the artist; he should be grateful that he is allowed to paint at all and is quite unreasonable to expect to be paid for doing what he likes. But we do not say that of other men who are getting pleasure out of their work and who are not nearly so useful to society.

To summarize, let us say that everyone has been at some time in his life a creative artist. A few continue to be so. The others not only lose their capacity to create, but are educated out of their capacity to feel and to appreciate. It is their duty toward the artist and toward themselves to strive to recover that capacity by reeducating themselves or unlearning their wrong education. All that most artists ask is to be understood and to give pleasure. In an ideally constituted society the potentially creative persons would not be forced into other professions. It is better to have thousands of bad artists and not to lose the few good ones who now get away from us.

Everyone is an artist. The man painting today is painting for you and instead of you. He is working for *you*. In the mystical sense in which the saints of old assumed the burden of the sins of others and found in doing so, not only suffering, but also a deep, spiritual joy, so the artist assumes the burden of expressing the emotions of mankind, and though this entails work and suffering, he, too, finds a joy in it. The artist is speaking for the race, for you and for me, and, in so doing, he liberates us from the narrow confines of our limited personality and reveals us to ourselves.

Who is the artist? Remember the lines of Donne which Hemingway made so well-known lately, "Send not to know for whom the bell tolls. It tolls for thee." In the same semi-mystical sense we can say, "Seek not to know the artist by name. The artist is you, yourself." In so far as the picture is felt deeply by you, it becomes a part of you; it expresses your deepest self, and through the medium of the picture there takes place a communion of artist and spectator which unites you forever.

4

WHAT DOES THE ARTIST DO?

What the artist does might be divided into
two parts, one of which we have already touched on to some
extent. First, what does the artist do *for* himself and society,
and second, what does he do *with* his hands and material?

For himself and society the artist performs a function some
aspects of which we have already mentioned. He organizes and
relates form so that the order of the universe becomes clear and
simplified and the relationship between objects and each
other, and between man and the external world, becomes
apparent. He fulfills man's basic urge to create, becoming a
vicarious creator for all men. He produces that which gives
man not only greater understanding of the world but also
delight and joy in various wide fields of experience. He

61

broadens our outlook by showing differing facets of many minds and feelings. He gives us wonder and excitement, even humor.

At its best a work of art can exalt to ecstasy, give a feeling of oneness with infinity. By *infinity* is meant the unity of all existing things, material, mental, and spiritual. Man's relationship with infinity, or totality, is important to man and the race. We must realize that the magnitude of the universe does not imply the smallness of man. Man is the highest development life has reached. Man has attained conscious power over his surroundings; he can change and develop himself and his environment. It is important that he change both in the right direction, toward a fuller, richer development. But we are straying too far afield. This is apropos of the subject of this chapter only in so far as it points up the fact that what each person does is important to the whole of mankind, and that a great responsibility rests upon the artist —to work sincerely and honestly. Few artists are capable of exalting us to ecstasy, but even those who are able to delight us, or even simply amuse us, must do it honestly and sincerely. Their work must be based on some universal principle of form and order.

Now as to what the artist does with his material and his hands.

In order to make clearer what the artist does, it would be well to return to child drawings and see how the problems of expression are dealt with on the earliest levels; then we can follow them in their development through the work of mature artists. The problems that the child faces in his first attempts at representation are the same as all artists face. His solution is the basis of, and points the way for, all later solutions.

The very earliest stages of development do not interest us here. It is at the schema stage that the foundation is laid on which is built the art of the mature painter. You might even say that this foundation is laid on scribbling, because without that stage the schema stage is impossible. But it is at the schema stage that the problems become clear. These problems that the child must deal with are tremendous and have challenged the greatest acuity and sensitivity on the part of the most advanced adult artists. The child has not only to devise adequate and satisfactory symbols to stand for his ideas of physical objects, but he must deal with the ideas of space, time, and the relationships between himself and objects and space and time. This would seem to be insuperably difficult; yet every child succeeds instinctively. His first step is to experiment until he evolves certain arrangements of marks on the paper that become for him satisfactory equivalents for his ideas of objects he sees about him. Let us stress the point that these equivalents or symbols stand, not for the object itself, but for the child's idea of the object. Symbol making occurs in three ways. Either a characteristic part of an object is used to stand for the whole object, as a round black spot, representing the pupil, may stand for the whole eye. Or a characteristic quality of the object may stand for the object, as a circle, roundness, may stand for a head. The third method of symbol making is less used by children than by adults, but it is well to mention it here. It is symbol making by transference. An instance of this is the flag of a country, which stands for the country by transference. Our emotions toward our country are aroused by the flag that stands for it. Another example of this type of symbolism is a coffin, which, by transference, recalls our feelings about death.

Man's greatest interest is in man, and therefore one of the first objects a child tries to draw is a human being. The parts of human beings he draws first are the parts that are important to him: the head, the eyes, the body, and the legs.

63

The size of these parts is dictated by the idea the child is trying to express, not by their relative sizes in nature. (See Plate IX.) Arms, hands, feet, etc., are added and accented only as they are needed to express an idea. For instance, a man running may have long legs and big feet, but no hands or arms. In a man reaching to pick fruit from a tree or throwing a ball, the legs may be reduced to mere rudimentary sticks, while the arms will be long, heavy, and important. The parts of the human body that are least used, and therefore least felt in action, such as the ears and the neck, are never drawn at all in the earlier schema stage and have little importance in the later. At first the child experiments with many different ways of representing a human being— heads may be drawn in many shapes; eye symbols will differ in each drawing—but finally he strikes a symbol which satisfies him for each part, and at this point symbols become schema. Schema is a rigid, crystallized system of symbols. Now the evolution of the child proceeds slowly and only in the direction of the addition of facts.

Let us see how this process occurs in a drawing of a human head. At the schema stage the child has evolved a symbol of a circle (roundness) to represent the head itself; two ovals with dots in the middle represent eyes; two dots close together stand for nose (by the symbol system of a characteristic part standing for the whole, in this case, the nostrils); a line is mouth. Those are the important facts about heads to a child at that stage. These symbols are invariable except as to size relationship, which is dictated by the idea the child wishes to express. For instance, the mouth of a man crying out will be large, or the eyes of a man staring at something will be exaggerated in size. This schema system will remain unaltered, but as the child develops in knowledge, he will add to his basic schema other facts he has noted. There will

64

appear a chin, which may be represented as a circle or half circle or triangle under the mouth; there will be eyebrows, ears, neck, forehead, the last often drawn as a square or circle above the eyes. Cheeks are felt and these are added, sometimes as circles, sometimes as dark spots. Hair appears, first as a scribble outside the head outline, then consisting of strokes in one direction, and finally shown as a dark, definite shape within the head outline. The nose, which started as two dots, is gradually realized as a triangle with the apex starting between the eyes. The single line of the mouth is divided into two lips. Details are added to the eye schema, lids, lashes, etc. At a certain point the child becomes aware of the profile and draws the head from that aspect, but since he knows that there are two eyes in a head and since that fact is important to him, he continues to draw both eyes in the profile head, and the whole mouth as well. In every stage of development we are reminded again and again that it is not what the child sees that he draws, but what he knows about the object. His drawing will be the same in every particular, whether he has the object he is portraying right before his eyes, or whether he is drawing it from memory.

Now it is clear that the child uses symbols that he invents to stand for his idea of the object he wants to portray. This is exactly what the adult artist has to do and by the very same mental process, except that the adult artist must consciously try to prevent his symbol system from becoming crystallized into a schema. He must try to remain supple and sensitive, so that the symbols he uses are imposed in every case, not by a preconceived mental system, but by his feeling at the time toward the object itself. He must devise each time he paints a picture the best, the most efficient, and the most economical symbols to express his emotion toward that object.

Let us now glance very briefly at how the child works out the problem of space and how this solution changes with added knowledge through various phases of experience. The methods of dealing with space used by the adult artist are founded upon the different solutions worked out at different stages of child development. By the time an adult has decided to become an artist, he has passed through many stages of artistic development; he is not starting from scratch. He knows so well his former solutions to many problems that he has forgotten that he knows them, which is the best kind of knowledge, the kind we have at our command automatically and constantly. The adult has established his relationship to space, but the child is in the process of establishing it.

The first relationship established is his own relationship with the earth he stands on. This is symbolized by a base line, and this base line retains its importance through all the stages of the child's development. Everything in the picture is related to and oriented by this base line. When a problem is presented which we would solve by the use of perspective, for example the portrayal of a street with trees on both sides, the base line becomes the median line, in this case the street, and the two rows of trees are drawn on each side of this line, growing away from it in opposite directions. This solution of the space problem is called *folding over* and it is a logical and legitimate solution, as much so as our more visual solution of perspective.

Objects behind each other never hide each other in a child's drawing. The visual fact that we do not actually see what is behind an object is of no interest or value to the child. Usually the object behind is drawn above the object in the foreground, and often it, too, has its base line, its own established relationship with the earth.

Size relationships are established on the principle of im-

66

portance. Again the visual illusion that objects look smaller the farther away they are does not matter.

One more of the many problems that must be solved by the child is interesting, though not so important to the adult artist as the problems of symbols and space. That is the problem of time. There may be two kinds of time in a picture: first, the time that elapses in the action portrayed; and, second, the time that the eye of the spectator takes in moving over the canvas. The first kind of time is the only one consciously dealt with by the child, and the latter is the only kind dealt with by adult artists today, but this difference was not always so, nor need it be so. It has only become a kind of artificial convention not to use the former kind of time, and it may be that a great artist will come along and revive this time element, which was used until fairly recently in art history, that is, up to the eighteenth century. The method used to express elapsed time in an action or series of actions is simply to portray in the same picture the same person in the various stages of his linked chain of activities. For instance, a man taking a journey is shown leaving the house, again boarding the train, again in the train, and finally getting out of the train at his destination. Many of the religious paintings of the lives of the saints use this storytelling device. The reason it has fallen into disuse today is that we no longer need to put art to the service of storytelling; today we can all read, and storytelling in pictures is no longer necessary.

Art through the ages has been associated in this arbitrary and superficial way with a number of man's activities—religion, morality, politics. There are even people today who feel that art has not the right to exist as an end in itself but must be linked to something else in order to justify itself. We shall go into that more fully when we talk about art and the spectator.

Symbols have been used by artists all through history and are used by artists today. The types of symbols used vary. Today each artist works out his own. In Egypt, Persia, and China the symbols crystallized into a schema; that is, they became rigid and invariable and were used by all artists over long generations. Space representation by means of base line and folding over have been used by adult artists of many lands and many periods. We have already mentioned the use of repetition devices to represent time. In the development of art in a country where it has had a long and continuous history, such as Egypt, art historians and ethnologists have tried to make comparisons between the way art evolves in races and the way it evolves in the individual. They have tried to prove that races pass through all the various stages that the individual passes through in reaching a mature art. It is an interesting subject for research and speculation, but much remains to be done before a parallel can be drawn.

The differences between what we have called the haptic type and the visual type are apparent almost from the beginning and become more marked as the art of the individual develops. The visual type naturally becomes more dependent upon the way things look; his interest centers more and more outside himself. The haptic never loses his sense of being the center of experience; the experience takes place in himself, and this is shown in his work by a closer relation of space to self or to the image which represents self. Size relationships are based on value judgments, not on visual size. *Value judgment* means that the objects or parts are important because of their emotional value, because they are more strongly felt. All children, as we have said, are more haptic than adults. The visual type becomes less and less haptic as he matures; that is, his bodily sensations become less important than the world around him. In the haptic type the shift of focus does

68

not take place or takes place only to a minor extent. There seem to be periods in history when haptic art is dominant, other periods when visual art plays the major role. Perhaps this is in response to some deep need in society. Possibly haptic art becomes important when man feels the need to aggrandize himself, to accentuate his individuality in a hostile world.

Another interesting difference in artist personality, which appears at the earliest stages of personal art development and continues throughout, is the difference in the work of boys and girls. This difference is consistent. Girls always draw things in a different way from boys. Different objects and parts are more important to them; heads and feet are smaller; eyes are larger; clothing is more accentuated. The fact of this constant difference is interesting in that it shows that art is based on the personality structure of the individual and that there is a consistent difference in the psychology of the sexes from the earliest days.

We mentioned in the last chapter that all children finally reach a crisis point at which art is abandoned by most people. In order to continue in art the artist must become conscious of basic techniques; he must experiment until he forges a personal means of expression which fits his thought and emotion so that they become fused into perfect unity. This demands all of an artist's best intelligence as well as extreme sensibility and long years of hard work. We often see painting in which the emotion motivating the work was evident, but the technique was not assimilated and calls attention to itself. Rule: The technique must be the simplest possible to express the content. Innumerable snags, obstacles, and traps stand in the way of an artist's arriving at the perfect expression. One might say he never arrives, because he is a growing and changing organism. As he matures, his art must also change and mature and he must find new means of expression.

There are also many examples of young artists who find a technique and who grow personally, but whose art remains static, or who perhaps do not themselves develop into full maturity. The art which at first was fresh and brilliant acquires the vitiated, pathetic quality we find in perpetual adolescents —those people whose bodies mature and wither, but who retain the outlook they had in their teens. A live art must grow with the man.

Let us put ourselves in the artist's place at the inception of a work of art and follow the process through as nearly as possible to the finished work. We start with two things, the artist and an object in the external world. The artist's eye sees this object, but before it enters into his mind, his eye makes a choice. The simplest object in nature is so complicated and so clustered round with associations that automatically and constantly our eye rejects what is not interesting or necessary to us. What the artist, or any one of us, registers in the mind and what we reject is decided by our early training, our condition at the moment, and many other factors. To give an example of what is meant by a temporary bodily condition influencing our seeing, a thirsty man will choose to see a glass of water, where another would see the roses that were standing in it. First an unconscious choice is made by the eyes. The image then enters perception—we know the object is there, we are conscious of it. Immediately upon perception, personality enters into the situation and tinges the perception with emotion. Next, the object becomes a concept; we relate it to other objects of the same kind, to our experiences of time and space. The concept rests on a fund of subconscious experiences and draws depth and richness from it. At this point, the stage of putting on canvas the emotions aroused by the impact of the external object on the mind of the artist, differences appear in the methods adopted

70

by artists in translating and externalizing these emotions. Some artists seem to see nature in the light of their inner vision of the world. These artists often think that they are copying nature and paint directly from it, but the result is distorted, impressed by their mental image. Others take material and arrange it with logical, conscious thought. Others, directed by the power of emotion, do not use the object before them except for notes or drawings or to refresh their mental vision. They combine pure mental image and emotion with the nature object.

The object before the artist strikes his eye and certain details and qualities of it enter his consciousness and become a *percept*. This enters his mind and is linked with a network of associations and knowledge formed by experiences with similar objects. An emotion is aroused, perhaps involving bodily sensations of the weight, the coolness, the feel of this object and similar objects handled and known in the past. Memory recalls facts and feelings, such as that this object has another side which cannot now be seen but is a part of the whole, that the shadow which now envelops one side of this object is a purely temporary phenomenon and not an intrinsic element of the object itself. At this point the artist begins to analyze, consciously or unconsciously. He tries to discover what aspects of this object give him the emotion he feels when he looks at it and what aspects are incidental and unnecessary to that emotion. Here a further process of simplification and elimination takes place. A purely mechanical elimination has already taken place by which the eye itself has eliminated certain details which were not important to it. This second elimination is quite conscious with some artists; with others it is more or less instinctive. Another thing that happens at this stage is an exaggeration or accentuation of the parts and elements of the object which have a bearing on the emotional response of the artist. This exaggeration may also be conscious or unconscious and usually takes one of two forms: the important aspect is accented either by an exaggeration of size or by a heightening of value contrast (light and dark) or of color.

Now the artist is standing before his canvas, a large, white, rectangular, flat surface. In his mind he has a picture which differs from the object he has been looking at in that it is simplified in some respects and elaborated or exaggerated in others. The artist is in a state of emotional tension, but his mind is alert; he is feeling and thinking. He will need all his wits about him for this task of putting on canvas his mental image.

What are his means for translating this emotional vision, which is purely a subjective thing, into painted forms on this white canvas before him, which is quite concrete? Art has a language whose grammar must be learned. It is by means of this art grammar that the artist must translate from the language of life into the language of art. His means are very few.

He has *line*, and a great deal can be expressed with a line. It can be made to bound a form, either a flat shape or a mass with depth, an illusionary three-dimensional form. It can be made to induce the eye of the spectator to move across the canvas in the direction the artist wishes. It can be made to express rhythm (through repetition, like the notes in music), harmony (through the relationship of one line to another), or balance. And, finally, it can be made to express an emotional state of mind by the quality of the line itself. It may be broken and jagged or smooth and flowing; it may be strong and vigorous or weak and nervous. This quality of line is very useful to the artist and is so closely linked to his very nerves and muscles that his excitement or his feelings of

72

peace and harmony will flow almost unconsciously from his finger tips through his brush. The line made by a man in a rage cannot be the same as that made by a calm man. Our very heartbeats influence the lines we make. Quality of line is very closely allied to the artist's emotional state and perhaps, with the exception of color, is the most instinctive expression of it. (See Plates X and XI.)

Next, the artist has *form* as a medium of expression, and in connection with form he must consider the relationships between one form and another and between forms and space. It is here, in the conception and arrangement of his forms, that the artist's greatest task lies. Here he shows his feeling of universal and harmonious relationships, of the eternal and underlying meaning behind the accidental aspects of things. He must lose the particular in the universal, show that this is not one individual object with its accidental peculiarities, but that it is the eternal essence of all objects of its kind. The relationships between the objects on the canvas must seem inevitable and complete. It must seem impossible to remove any detail without destroying the unity of the picture. The artist knows that the object before him, the real object that he is translating into the language of art, exists in one world, whereas he is creating a new object and at the same time creating a new world in which this new object exists. Therefore he takes from the real object only those qualities which can be transmuted in his mind into this new material, and in the process he has the right to use any means he can to attain his end. He may eliminate, distort, exaggerate. (See Plate XIX.) In the arrangement of the forms on the canvas the artist has again to consider rhythm, harmony, and balance.

We have just said that the artist's sense of his own relationship with the universe is expressed through his arrangement of forms and space. A man with a sense of insecurity in

73

the world will have a tendency to fill his spaces, to crowd his shapes together, to leave no frightening open spaces. A man with a feeling of the magnitude of the universe in comparison with infinitesimal man will have a tendency to paint large open spaces, in which objects lose their size and importance.

Space itself is equal in importance to objects. The adjustment between the two makes a picture. Space must have a shape, and this shape must be pleasing and must be related to the shapes of the objects. However, the boundaries of space are also the boundaries of the objects, and the eye must be deluded into imagining a continuation of this space behind the object and only unconsciously consider the shapes of the various parts of it.

The last technical tool that the artist has at his command with which to create a picture is *color*. Color seems to react more directly upon the senses than either line or form. We react to color in the same way as we react to music, and, in fact, color can be compared quite closely to music. There are color "tones" and "harmonies" and even color "scales." Color in a picture must obey the fundamental laws of rhythm, harmony, and balance, but its main function seems to be to set a tonality of mood in the spectator. Closely related colors in a somber key would not be used by the artist in a picture of a gay country dance, such as Breughel's "Country Fair," nor the bright and contrasted tones of a Matisse in a painting of the Crucifixion. Color, besides setting a mood tone, arouses a sensuous delight in the eye; the actual vibrations of color give us pleasure. There have been artists, Kandinsky among others, who took such delight in color for its own sake that they felt no need for the use of definite forms and lines. Their compositions are merely vague movements of color, which charm us while the eye dwells on them but do not penetrate beneath the senses. They leave the deep inner ·

74

man untouched. There have been very great artists with little or no color sense. Michelangelo is an example. A feeling for form seems to be an essential of great painting, but it is possible to be a great painter with little or no feeling for color. However, the ideal painter would be the man who combines all the possible means—line, form, and color—and equally develops and utilizes them.

Now let us come back to our artist standing before his canvas and see what he has been doing. There is now on the canvas before him an organization of lines, either forming boundaries of forms and spaces, or utilized for themselves alone to direct the eye of the spectator in a given direction, and expressing through their quality of smooth flow or their nervous roughness the emotional condition of the artist. There are forms which are related to each other and to spaces, forms which are expressive of the artist's feeling about life and of his attitude toward the world he lives in. These forms usually suggest weight and sometimes strain or tension, and in so far as they do so, we, in looking at them, react in our very nerves and muscles. The way the artist has painted these forms, his manner of putting on the paint, his brush strokes, even, may suggest the softness or hardness of objects, their coolness or warmness. These forms may embody more facts than are visible in the original "real" object, facts that we or the artist know about the object or similar objects from former experiences. Last of all, the artist has employed color in tones of darks and lights to fashion his forms and spaces and has heightened the emotional content of the picture by this means.

Up to this point the artist has been a creator, but now he must double as a critic. It is impossible to be both at once, but after the artist has expressed on canvas his emotional state and is therefore emptied of it, he must call up all his knowl-

75

edge, all his understanding, all his past learning to compare and correct. Here is where many artists fail. They can create, but they cannot act the critic toward their own work.

With what, then, does the artist compare his newly created work? With the "real" object which was the starting point for his picture? Not at all. That object no longer has any relationship to the work of art which has just been produced. Whether the picture is like or unlike it is completely beside the point. The artist first compares his picture with his mental image, with his original conception, and then he compares it with his own former work to see whether he has made progress in self-expression, and finally he compares it with the painting of other artists of the past to see whether it is worthy of a place in the hierarchy of the great art of all times.

Most artists find that an immediate judgment is difficult. The mental image which they have been trying to translate into paint is still so strong in their minds that it mixes with and is superimposed upon the actual work of art before them. They see a composite picture, resulting from the mixture of this mental image and what is actually on the canvas. Therefore they put the picture away for a week or a month or a year and review it again when the mental image has faded and when they can more coldly appraise the work of art. If it then comes up to their standards, they put it in the best frame they can afford and send it out into the world of art dealers and exhibitions. From then on the rest is up to you.

This description of an artist creating a work of art is true only to the extent that a description of the "average" man is true. Into this framework must be fitted the infinite variety of actual human personalities.

In what directions does this creative process vary with individuals? The first possibility of variation is in the actual conception of the picture. We have said that our artist sets up an object—it may be a still life of flowers, or an old man, or a sunset, or anything else in the visible world that is capable of arousing an emotional response—and from this object he extracts the materials employed in the creation of his picture. He does this by a more or less conscious process of elimination and simplification of certain aspects of the object and by the exaggeration of others. But there are certain human beings, and not all artists, either, who have the capacity at times to see nature as a work of art, to see an object as a stark reality in itself, stripped of all associations; they see it in its universal reality, not as a mental concept in the mind, but actually with the bodily eyes. This capacity, which comes and goes, must be similar to the visions of the mystics who see at times a sudden glory in the world before them, so that the world for them is changed from the drabness of utilitarianism and action into a world of eternal beauty and truth. For these people, when they happen to be artists, the first step of converting a visual reality into a mental concept of universal import is unnecessary. It is already done for them, and they will tell you that they copy what they see. But what they see is not what you and I see.

Then there are other ways of creating a work of art besides working from an object directly before the eyes. There are artists who work from memory. Time does the eliminating and simplifying. This type of artist may use a memory of one experience or a composite memory of many experiences. There are also artists whose starting point is pure imagination and whose pictures are rearranged into forms and ideas existing only in a world of fantasy. And there are the surrealists, who use very concrete objects in relationships and proportions which are impossible in our life experience, but which occur only in their dream life.

We have already said that there are two types of artists,

77

one for whom the visual predominates, and one for whom the bodily sensations have the greatest importance. Either of these types may begin the composition of a picture in any of the above ways. In the haptic type the tone of feeling is set by the knowledge he has gained through experience of the tactile values of the objects before him or the strain of muscles in his body in response to a seen or even imagined movement. To this man it is not the redness nor the light on a rose that is important. It is the softness and the coolness of the petals, the weight of the blossom which bends the stem. He may even feel in his own body the pull that the stem might feel as it bends under that weight.

In the actual, concrete composition of a picture, when the image which the artist has in his mind is translated into line, form, and color, there are even more variations in possible methods of procedure than occur in the stage of conception.

To Artist A, for example, this process is as mysterious as it is to you and me. He stands before his canvas, paint-brush in hand, and his subconscious mind takes control of the situation, while his conscious mind steps aside, as it were, and waits. The painting appears on the canvas in the same way that automatic writing appears on a sheet of paper when a man is under hypnosis. In the case of the hypnotized person the very muscles of the hand know the formation of letters because of years of practice in writing, and so in the case of the artist the hand must know the language of art. Long years of training must have made this technique a natural and automatic response. A well-trained pianist cannot hit a wrong note; his fingers themselves know. He does not think, I will reach A with the first finger and D with the fourth. His fingers automatically strike the notes. So it is with Artist A. His long years of training have resulted in such a well-worn channel of nerve and muscle responses that it has sunk below the conscious level; it takes care of itself. When his painting is finished, he may stand back and look at it and say with surprise, "I did not intend to paint this." But the real Artist A, the deep, dark, inner Artist A, did intend it. It is exactly what he intended.

At the other end of the scale we have Artist Z, who knows consciously every moment what he is up to. He may even verbalize as he works and say to himself, "I need a diagonal there to lead the eye across the canvas. This form must be balanced by that. There should be greater emphasis here to concentrate the attention."

Between Artist A, whose subconscious only is in control, and Artist Z, who works with a complete consciousness of the rules and techniques involved, we have the whole alphabet of painters who work at times consciously, at others unconsciously, or who alternate periods of instinctive creation with periods of critical clarity.

With nearly all artists there is a point at which the picture comes alive. At first the attention or interest of the artist is concentrated on the object before him or on his mental concept, his memory, or fantasy. His first arrangements of line on the canvas usually do not correspond exactly to that image. He moves these lines to right or left, nearer or farther from each other, subtly altering their relationships; sometimes he effaces them partially or completely; sometimes he is almost blindly feeling his way with his brush by instinct. Then suddenly the pattern before him begins to have meaning, to suggest a unified whole. From this point on, every stage in the process of completion is influenced by what is on the canvas more than by what was in the artist's mind or before his eyes. The picture itself grows inevitably from one established stroke to the next. Sometimes the result is very far from both the original object and the artist's concept.

What we have called the language of art has, like actual

verbal language, both grammar and meaning. We may know English grammar perfectly and be incapable of understanding profound or technical ideas expressed in that language. To understand ideas we must have a basis in ourselves for that comprehension, we ourselves must be profound. This is a matter of personal growth which comes about slowly, by a process of contact with great minds and gradual assimilation and maturity. The fostering of this growth is up to the individual himself. He must find the food he needs; it is all about him, and only he himself can tell what his hunger is at the moment. In the case of art development, the food for the spirit is works of art and there is an abundance of all kinds for all spiritual needs. But, to return to our language simile, without some knowledge of grammar ideas cannot be imparted.

It may be of some help if we review briefly the grammar of art. Line, form, and color (including dark and light, sometimes called *chiaroscuro*, from the Italian word meaning light-dark) are the parts of speech of the artist's language. Rhythm, harmony, and balance (including contrast) are his means of grouping them to convey ideas. He must take line, form, and color and arrange them in a pattern of rhythm, harmony, and balance. Simple, isn't it? It is like saying that a writer must take nouns, verbs, and adjectives and arrange them in a sentence with a subject and a predicate. However, we must never lose sight of the fact that this alone is not what makes him a writer.

Let us look at some of the ways in which painters have arranged their material, at a few out of the infinite number of possible ways of composing a picture. It seems convenient for analytical purposes to divide pictures into those that are flat and those that have depth. Actually all pictures are flat, the canvas itself is flat, so that when we speak of depth in a picture, we are speaking of an illusion, of the expression of a *feeling*

80

of depth arrived at by technical tricks. This illusion is concentrated in the eye of the spectator. It is his eye alone that enters the canvas, and the illusion of distance may cause the focusing muscles of the eye to react. It is the artist's business to control this effect. He must not allow the eye to enter the picture deeper and deeper, to infinity, with no way back. The spectator must not be plunged into a bottomless abyss of space. No, the eye must be led. It must enter the canvas at a certain point, be allowed to attain a certain depth, be coaxed back a certain distance, then in again, perhaps several times, rhythmically, and finally led safely to the surface. The depth to which the eye is allowed to plunge varies with different pictures by different artists, but it must always be strictly controlled, and if this journey into depth is skillfully managed by the artist, the eye itself receives a pleasure from the rhythmic muscle movements involved. It can be a kind of dance of the eyes.

What about "flat" paintings? In this type of painting, too, it is the artist's business to lead the spectator's eyes on a rhythmic journey, but instead of leading them in and out of the canvas, he leads them only over the surface. In a picture which has no illusion of depth, therefore no feeling of three-dimensional masses, line becomes the most important element. It is line that must be used to lead the eye. The spectator must be induced to enter the picture at a certain point, to journey along a certain route, to arrive finally at the point where the most interesting things are happening, to dwell there for a time, and then to leave by a convenient path. On this visual journey all sorts of exciting, unexpected, soothing, or poetical things may happen. One of the ways of pleasing and interesting the eye lies in the quality of the line. We have already noted that a line can be expressive of mood and emotion. It can be broken, jerky, quavering; it can

81

feel its way along slowly, delicately; it can move in passionate darts or sweeps; it can be hard and direct, or broad and flowing. The eye moves along it in the direction and at the speed the artist wills, and here again the means of rhythm, harmony, and balance are employed.

Rhythm is repetition of a motive or motives in a recognizable pattern. "Ordered movement by relations is rhythm," says Walter Abell. In the case of painting, this means ordered movement of the eye. The simplest form of rhythm is a single motive repeated at regular intervals. Our interest in that kind of rhythm soon palls; if it continues too long, boredom ensues; if it continues beyond the point of boredom, it can drive us to madness. You remember the Emperor Jones and the monotonous drumbeat. There must be enough variety in the lines or groups of lines that are repeated and in the intervals between them to avoid boredom. We must be led to expect an exact repetition and then pleasantly disappointed by being presented with a variation or with a different motive altogether, one which we would never have thought of but which is related to the preceding motives in a way that we recognize with a shock of surprise.

Here we touch on an important element in art which links it psychologically with humor. Max Eastman, in his *Enjoyment of Laughter*, says that the basis of humor is disappointment. We are led to expect a certain effect or result and then either deprived of it or presented with another, unexpected one instead. The resulting shock leads to laughter and a release of nervous tension. The same means used in art results, not in laughter, but in a refreshing shock. We are given, for example, a rhythmic succession of curves, and when we are quite relaxed and prepared to continue this soothing rise and fall, we are suddenly brought up short by a reverse curve. The

82

motive introduced by way of variation must, however, be of the same kind as the preceding series.

For instance, let us draw a parallel in another field. If we have a series of numbers—let us say the numbers 1-2 repeated like this: 1-2, 1-2—we may vary the repetitive pattern by introducing either the number 3, which is related to 1 and 2 by being next in a series and also by being the sum of the two preceding numbers, or by the number 4, which is number 2 doubled, as 2 is number 1 doubled. Or we may use a number related in other ways to the preceding 1 and 2. But we could not introduce at this point a letter, for instance, or, still less, a geometrical form.

So in art, if the rhythm is linear, the variation introduced must be linear; it cannot be form or color; and it must be different, but not too different in quality and direction. Our mind must be able to make the connection between all the parts. We must see the relationship almost immediately after the shock of surprise. This shock of surprise is a most important element in a picture. We should say to ourselves, "I never would have thought of that, I never would have done that." If we do not say this, consciously or unconsciously, if the picture is just what we ourselves would have done had we been artists, we are getting no new experience, and we may be sure that we are looking at the same old secondhand materials of art rewarmed.

To return to line and its function in a painting, we repeat that its main purpose is to move the eye across the canvas. When we speak of movement in relation to a work of art, we always mean the directed movement of the eye and not, of course, the movement or action portrayed in the represented figures. There can be a great deal of excited movement in a picture of apples lying on a table, and the picture of a man running may be perfectly static. It is the artist's business to control movement of the eye across the canvas. He must not allow us to cross the canvas with express-train rapidity, nor must we come to a dead end or backwash where we are dropped and cannot move. We must be kept going into every part of the canvas, now faster, now slower, pausing to enjoy the variations and complexities of the more important parts, speeding up on our rhythmic journey over the less important areas, sensing and enjoying the variations in line quality, in rhythm, in direction, and finally we must be allowed to leave, refreshed and renewed.

Line has another very important function in a canvas besides that of controlling the movement of the eye. Line also bounds forms. In nature line in this sense does not exist. What we see as the boundary of forms in nature changes if we move our heads an inch to one side or the other. The object continues behind and beyond the edge we happen to be seeing at the moment. That edge is not actually a line but only the point beyond which we happen at the moment not to be able to see. But in art line is the means we have for delimiting forms. If these forms are flat, with little or no illusion of depth and weight, the line that defines them assumes a greater importance, the outline of the shape is accented. If the picture is composed by masses with weight and depth, the core of those masses is the important thing. It expresses their feeling from the inside out, the forms as a solid unit. Solid forms, then, have to take over the function of line in moving the eye; the axis of the form determines the direction of the movement, and the shape, the weight, and the surface of that form control the speed at which the eye moves. In general, one can make the rule that the more depth and mass in a picture, the less important does line become, but there are many exceptions to this generalization. We have

84

artists who combine line and mass, using line either to limit the masses or in combination with them, and creating an arrangement of linear and mass contrasts. We have the purely linear, in which the lines in themselves are the pattern and suggest interior forms little, if at all; and we have compositions in pure mass whose edges are practically nonexistent and seem to melt into the background and continue around and behind the object. Renoir is a good example of this type of nonlinear painting.

It might be useful here to repeat what we have said before: that the elements used by the painter are line, form, and color, and that the means employed in their arrangement are rhythm, harmony, and balance. Line must have rhythm, harmony, and balance, and so must form and color. We have considered rhythm in relation to line, where it is most easily applied and most readily discerned. We have no difficulty in following a succession of pulsating curves or a repetition of similar angles. When it comes to forms, our associative memory rises and obscures the relationships between similar forms with dissimilar associations. In other and plainer words, we find it difficult to realize that the shape of a tree trunk in the background of a picture is a rhythmic repetition of the shape of a man's leg in the foreground and the shape of a cloud in the sky. We associate clouds with clouds and trees with trees but not shapes with shapes.

The same management of rhythmic repetitions is used in the arrangement of color on the canvas; the same or similar values and hues are repeated and varied in order to create a moving or pleasing pattern. By *value* in color is meant the degree of light or dark of a certain color; thus a low value of blue is a dark blue and a high value, a light blue. By *hue* is meant the color itself in relation to other colors of the spectrum, its identity as green or blue or orange. There is a third possible variation in color besides its value and hue, and that is its *intensity*, or the degree of grayness. A pure color is of the highest intensity, a very grayed color of the lowest. Intensity means the purity of a color. You may have a hue of low value and high intensity, of high value and low intensity, or any variation between these extremes. The colors themselves are divided into *cold* and *warm*. The more blue a color contains, the colder; the more orange it contains, the warmer. This gives us still another possibility of rhythmic arrangement that is particularly useful in rhythms in depth, when the artist wishes to lead the eye into and out of the canvas. Blue has the property of retreating. It gives the illusion of distance, no doubt an association with the distant sky or the blue haze of the far mountains and horizons. Orange advances. A proper arrangement, therefore, of cold and warm tones can help the artist to control the depth to which he wishes the eye to penetrate and the intervals of that penetration.

Color, while it is an extremely important element in the composition of a picture, cannot be conceived apart from form. Color and form are inseparable. We cannot think of a color without a form. Even the vast blue of the sky is bounded by the roof we see against it or by the wide circle of the edge of the world. We can conceive of a form without color, but not of a color without form.

We have considered now the possibilities of rhythmic arrangements of line, form, and color. Rhythm seems to be a repetition of single or grouped elements with variations introduced to form a recognizable pattern. We have gone into the application of rhythm to the composition of a picture in some detail, because much of what has been said is also true of balance and harmony, the other two means at the artist's disposal.

In order to understand what is meant by *balance* in a paint-

86

ing, let us put ourselves again in the artist's place, standing before a rectangular, white canvas. We have to fill this flat shape with line, form, and color. For the moment we shall put aside the question of emotional expression and consider our task from a purely technical viewpoint. Naturally we shall not cover one part of the canvas with a mass of interesting detail and leave the rest empty. Our natural instinct would make us feel that the canvas was too heavy on the filled side and too light on the empty side. There must be a center of balance, which is usually, though not necessarily, near the center of the canvas. This center or focal point acts as the fulcrum of a pair of old-fashioned balance scales. On both sides of this point there must be an equivalent.

The simplest example of balance is a bisymmetrical design, both sides of a center line being identical. But this is almost never used in a painting. It is too limiting and too simple to interest us. If we place on one side of our canvas a form that gives us the feeling of a certain weight, we must place something on the other side that seems to weigh as much. Here line, form, and color become interchangeable as to value, or weight; they become equivalents. For instance, we may use a large, light-colored, grayish form on one side of our scales, or our canvas, if you prefer, and we may decide to balance it with a small, dark, brightly colored shape. The greater intensity, hue, and value of the smaller object have compensated for the size of the larger object. Or we may substitute line for size, balancing our large simple form with a smaller one full of linear complexities.

If we wish to balance two forms, a large and a small, both of the same importance as to color and line, we have another recourse. We can place the smaller shape farther from the central fulcrum and the larger shape nearer it. This works in a picture in exactly the same way that it works on the scales when we move the smaller balancing weight out from the center on the longer arm of the scale in order to balance a heavier weight nearer the center on the opposite side. How far from the center the form should be, is a matter of its size and the feeling we have—we simply keep moving it farther from the center until we feel that it balances.

We must not forget that our scale works up and down on our canvas, as well as from side to side. The top of a picture must balance the bottom; if we turn our picture sideways and look at it, we must not feel too great a weight in the foreground which might pull the background over. However, we are allowed a little greater weight at the bottom of the picture. This carefully controlled heaviness at the base has a stabilizing effect. One thing we must not lose sight of is that the space, as well as the form, has shape and weight and must always be reckoned with in our weighing and balancing.

So far we have been talking about balance in connection with weight, which is primarily a nonvisual matter. Our whole idea of weight comes from a knowledge gained through our muscles, from the actual experience of lifting. There is another important aspect of balance that the artist must deal with, the balance of meaning or idea. We have said that the part of a picture that the artist feels of greatest importance will be accented by an elaboration of detail or an exaggeration of size. But there are certain things in life that interest us in themselves, that have for human beings a great natural attraction. The foremost of these is human beings themselves. If we have before us a chair or a tree and a person, our interest will be concentrated on the person; to us he is far more interesting than the tree or the chair. And in looking at a human being, the part to which our eyes are naturally attracted is his face. And, to continue, the part of his face

88

with the greatest attraction and interest for us is his eyes. In a picture of a landscape with a man, the man has the greatest importance of "meaning" or "idea." His figure will draw our eyes naturally, not because the artist has contrived it so by an elaboration or exaggeration, but by an innate human trait. If we have before us a painting of a full-length figure, our eyes will focus naturally on the face. If we have the painting of a head only, the eyes will be our natural center of interest. Thus, by a balance of idea or meaning is meant that the artist must take into consideration this natural human tendency to give value to certain objects or parts of objects, and the value and interest they have for us must be counterbalanced by something else of interest, or they must be so placed on the canvas that the different parts of the same object (a face for instance) balance each other.

If, for example, a painter for some reason or another wishes to place a figure at the extreme right-hand side of his canvas, he must, in contriving the balance of his picture, take into consideration, not only the physical weight of this figure, but also the psychological interest we have in it, and his counterbalance must be strong in interest, as well as in weight. In the case we are imagining, of a figure placed at the extreme right-hand edge of the canvas, the artist might use a number of tricks (or technical contrivances) to balance it. He might use elaboration of detail, exaggeration of size, accentuation of color, strong contrast of darks and lights. He might also use the psychological method of turning the face or eyes of the figure toward the object he has placed on the opposite side of his canvas. Our interest will follow the interest of the painted figure.

One more way of balancing a picture must be considered by the artist: the balance of contrast. In order to contrast one thing with another, both must belong to a series; they must be alike in kind but at opposite ends of a scale. For instance, one can contrast black with white or hot with cold; one cannot contrast black with cold. The artist may balance red with green by contrast, or dark with light, or triangles with curves.

There is not much that we need say about balance of color in a picture. All that we have said about balance of form applies to balance of color. Color must be balanced in its hue, its value, and its intensity.

Rhythm, balance, and harmony—these are the artist's means of expression, and the greatest of these is harmony. *Harmony* is the principle that controls the unity of a picture; it is the relationship of the various parts to each other. In speaking of balance, we are speaking of equivalents, but two things that are equal are still two separate things. It is the artist's job, in his composition of a picture, to bring these separate things into a relationship that creates a larger whole. This principle is sometimes called *unity,* and the task of the artist has been summarized as the attainment of variety in unity.

In a perfectly composed picture every element is so closely and inevitably related to every other that if a single detail were removed, the whole thing would collapse. It is only through this harmonious relationship of parts, which creates a unified whole, that the artist can hold us in this new world that he is presenting to us. We must not be allowed to stray away from it or be thrown back on ourselves or on the world until the experience the artist has to communicate is complete. Everything on the canvas must contribute to this experience, and all the means used must be tightly integrated and essential to it. Line must be closely related to form; form and color must be inseparable.

In general, one can make the rule that the simplest and

90

most economical way of expression is the best, that the means employed should be the absolute minimum possible to communicate the experience. Richness and elaboration for their own sake detract from the emotional impact. In poetry the simplest, clearest means of expression are the most moving, provided that the words chosen are exactly right. Too many or too fancy words confuse or bore us. In a picture, detail and elaboration must serve an essential purpose; they must be necessary to force the eye to pause where the artist wishes, or they must heighten the force of an individual part of the whole, but must never detract from that whole or become important for themselves alone.

We find, as we put ourselves in the artist's place and stand before our canvas, brush in hand, that our task is not the comparatively simple one of copying what we see before us. First of all, our eye makes a choice for us of the innumerable facts about the object we are looking at, a choice dictated by our past habits and experiences. Then our mind makes a further choice from the many facts delivered to it by the eye and relates these facts to universal principles or categories. The emotion aroused in us by the impact of this object combines with our previous knowledge of this object and others of its kind or related to it, knowledge that has been acquired through the sense of touch or muscle sensations or even through taste or smell. At this point some of us have a clear mental picture, ready to be translated into the language of art and put on canvas; some have only an emotional mental tone which extends below the conscious into the subconscious mind and is strong enough to control hand and brush in the work they must perform. And now, in order to express what we have to say, we utilize the grammar of art. We arrange line, form, and color into patterns of rhythm, balance, and harmony.

91

When we have finished, we judge our picture, not on the basis of the success of our use of these pictorial elements, not on our clever handling of rhythm, not on a satisfactory balance, not on a complete and inevitable unity, but only on the basis of our success or failure to express our emotional state and to impart it to the spectator. Just as a poet may write a perfect poem from the technical standpoint, with all his trochees and dactyls correct, and yet the poem may have value only as a model for a grammar student; so a painter may paint a technically perfect picture that means nothing. On the other hand, a very great painter can break one or all of the rules, and the force of his personality reaches us in spite of it.

Rules are made after the fact. After the artists have painted their pictures, along come the pedants and figure out how they did it and formulate the rules. This has been going on for centuries now, and the rules of rhythm, balance, and harmony have been found to be generally the basis of good art. There are artists who can and do ignore one or the other, though not all of these rules, and who still succeed in their primary task of moving us emotionally. What we ask of the artist is to lift us out of our narrow shells of selfhood, to present us with a complete and harmonious world in which the ego can rest in the assurance of being a part of a meaningful whole. If the artist does this for us, we shall not quibble with him over the means that he employs.

5

WHAT IS MODERN ART?

What kind of painting do you do?" This is
the first question that an artist is asked as soon as the hostess
has introduced him, "My friend A. He is an artist." The first
time he hears it, in his early youth, the question rocks him
back on his heels and causes a good deal of quick heart
scarching. Eventually he discovers that the question does not
mean "Do you do good painting or bad painting?" but
"Which of the convenient, man-made mental pigeonholes
can I fit your work away into so that I don't have to think
about it again?" And the artist works out a formula of some
sort to satisfy his questioner, such as "I paint landscapes," or
"I am an abstract artist."

If this conversation is taking place at an average American

dinner party, the artist who confesses that he does modern or abstract painting will be conscious of a strong reaction among the guests. Some will eye him with mistrust and antagonism and give him a wide berth for the whole evening. Others will corner him and attack him aggressively, as though he had personally insulted them. A few will try to find out from him what modern art is all about. Outside of the rather small groups of people who accept anything new because it *is* new, the general reaction in this country to modern art is still one of antagonism and almost of fear. There is also a strong element of bewilderment fostered by such books as *Mona Lisa's Mustache*, which accuses the modern artist of pulling a tremendous hoax on the public. It is strange that these attitudes of fear, antagonism, and bewilderment still exist in these times of the rapid spread of ideas, because modern art has existed for fifty years or more. The most revolutionary steps were taken in the first decade of this century.

It is characteristic of Americans to accept the new in everything material, in gadgets, cars, architecture. We have free, open, forward-looking minds. Wrong education is the only reason that we are so loath to accept the new in art. We are fearful of anything that strays from the old Renaissance formulas. We have been brought up to believe that art is old, dull, and found in museums. We are presented with a clutter of boring information, dates, and anecdotes about the painters. The point of view that art is a living experience, an *invention*, would make the exhibition of a new work of creative art as exciting as the preview of the new cars every year.

The bewilderment aroused by modern art is increased by the labels that have been attached to every local variation in its theories. Sometimes these names are given by the groups of artists who banded together to explore new possibilities,

94

sometimes by writers or critics who developed theories taken up by groups of artists, sometimes by the public to distinguish a trend. When we say we do not like modern art, do we mean that we do not like analytic or synthetic cubism, Fauvism, Dadaism, futurism, expressionism, constructivism, vorticism, syntheticism, Orphism, synchronism, suprematism, nonobjectivism, neoplasticism, purism, surrealism? Confusing, isn't it? Especially so as some of this flock of isms are diametrically opposed in method and in aim.

After peacefully developing for several hundred years along the lines of a visual approach to nature, something happened toward the end of the nineteenth century that started artists experimenting, reappraising, analyzing. The result has been probably the greatest resurgence of art ideas and the greatest development of new techniques since the Italian Renaissance. It is exciting to live in such times, and if we do not participate, we are missing a thrilling experience that few people in history have been privileged to share.

What was the happening that incited this ferment in art? Actually it was not one thing but many, and they happened in the realms of science and invention and changed the thinking and the lives of all of us.

The first of the discoveries to have a particular influence on art was research in the science of optics and color. We all know now that color is vibration, moving light rays that react upon the nerves of the eye, and that the color we see is simply the light rays that are bounced back off an object and not absorbed by it. It follows that with a change in position of the source of the light rays, or a change in the atmosphere (the layers of air enveloping the earth), or a change in the surrounding color, the appearance of color in an object will vary. As the scientists published their discoveries in the realm of light and optics, the group of artists who were later dubbed impressionists applied these various theories to painting.

At about the same time inventors and scientists were developing photography, which has had a tremendous effect upon painting in a variety of ways. It caused a reappraisal on the part of artists of the whole conception and purpose of art. For several hundred years the main current of art had been concerned with realism, and the only advance or change that art had made was in the direction of a more complete or exact representation of visible objects. There were individual artists who had a clearer picture of the meaning of artistic creation, and there were diverging currents and eddies of a more decorative or imaginative art, but on the whole the official view of painting was that it was an imitation of nature. Now, suddenly, the camera could do, in a few seconds and mechanically, a better job of reproducing what we see than any artist could ever do. What all great artists had either consciously known or subconsciously felt, that art was a creative process of the individual and not a mechanical reproduction of nature, became apparent to all. If reproduction was the artist's function, the camera put him out of business. Photography has since had other major effects upon painting. The discovery of microphotography showed us new forms and aspects of the world never before seen by man. These micro-forms have been used by many modern painters. We even see amoeba forms in advertising art now. Through the camera's eye we have been enabled to see the surfaces of moon and stars, to see life on earth from angles impossible to the human eye, to analyze objects in motion. A movement much too fast for the human eye to record can be arrested by the camera. We have been able to see plants growing and to see life under the seas. Thus there have been presented to the artist vast new funds of forms.

The discovery that color is not an intrinsic part of an

96

object, but is the effect of light rays reflected from that object, was only the beginning of a general undermining of the belief in the reality and stability of the world we see. Einstein and the physicists have shaken this old conception of the world still more, until now we all know that the objects around us, formerly thought of as solid and real, are actually a collection of electrical discharges in violent movement. Meanwhile two world wars have shaken our belief in the stability of governments and in the values which for centuries seemed inalterable. It is no wonder that the rapid changes that have taken place in the last fifty years, with all their shocks to the human psyche, have been reflected in the arts, a sensitive seismograph of the general culture and thinking of the people.

In the same fifty years that saw such great developments in science and invention, our whole way of life has been changed by the invention of machines from a handicraft to an industrial civilization. Mass production and the assembly line have changed man's age-old attitude toward his work. The machine itself has demonstrated new functional forms and movements. The invention of the automobile and the airplane have changed our conception of space and time and aroused an interest in movement and speed in relation to our lives and to art. All these things have started artists thinking in a direction away from realism, that is, towards abstraction.

We have seen that the development from realism to nonrealism is a matter of degree. All painting is to some extent nonrealistic. Exact reproduction of nature on a two-dimensional surface is impossible. The degree to which a picture is nonrealistic is determined by the amount of abstraction that the artist has contrived.

Exactly what is abstraction? Rudolph Arnheim in *Per-*

ceptual Abstraction and Art says, "[Abstract paintings] present types of objects, their general meaning rather than individual cases only. They represent visual reality in a simplified fashion." Samuel Johnson defined abstraction as "a smaller quantity containing the virtue or power of a larger." There is nothing very abstruse about that; in fact it seems as though abstract painting should be easier to understand than realistic painting, since it is a simplification of the material around us. Realistic art is actually more alien to our natural way of thinking and our instinctive manner of creating than is symbolic or abstracted art.

But what of the pictures that are simplified beyond recognition, in which we no longer see any connection with visual life? Just as there is no "realistic" painting that is not partly abstract, so there is no "abstract" painting that is not partly realistic. It is all a question of degree. How far into abstraction an artist goes and how far we can follow him with pleasure depends upon our nature and training. There is no point in the process of abstraction at which one can say "This far and no farther is it permitted to go away from life." We must realize that even the most geometric pictures, in which no relationship to life objects can be distinguished, are based on visual forms. Visual forms are all the artist has to work with, and only what he sees does he know. With this material his mind plays. He can combine their various parts and so make something new that has never existed before, or he can eliminate and condense, but the basic material with which he starts out is something seen in life.

We may lay down these precepts at the beginning of this chapter: All art is abstract to some degree. All art created in our time is modern, if only in a chronological sense. There is no such thing as purely nonrepresentational painting.

Nowadays we have the strange situation of a complete

98

noncomprehension of the more abstracted forms of art on the one hand and a strong tendency of art toward abstraction on the other hand. There is always a lag between the most creative artists and the public. Because of the imperfect dissemination of pictures, we, the public, do not see enough art to be able to feel and to judge the quality of artists who are working in a new idiom. It takes time to understand a new thing. In a previous chapter we mentioned that at various times in history art had passed through periods of greater or less abstraction. We seem now to be passing through a period in which there is a psychological need for abstract art. Although abstract, modern, or nonrepresentational art is only one manifestation of the art spirit, it seems to be a natural idiom of our day. It will probably be seen in retrospect from some future hill of time as a distinct, peculiar school or manner of our century. The lag, however, between artist and layman prevents many of us from understanding and appreciating this idiom; it is a difficulty for many of us, even the most cultivated and intelligent.

It is necessary to make a historical beginning in our discussion of modern art. This will be like fixing a point in a stream of running water. One artist leads to the next. All art is based on the preceding art, being either built on it or a reaction from it. But we shall arbitrarily select Cézanne as our beginning point. We shall try to show what he attempted to do and how he started modern painters thinking along certain lines.

No sooner do we fix a point for a historical beginning of modern art than we find it necessary to sketch in a base or background. Without the work of the impressionists, it is doubtful whether Cézanne would have painted as he did. And behind the impressionists are the romanticists, from whom the impressionists were reacting, and behind the romanticists,

99

the classicists. The progression was this: the development of a technique or idea until it became repetitive and dead, then a reaction from it and new paths to explore and develop.

Up to the time of the impressionists, color had been considered as a quality of an object; that is, a dress was red, a tree was green. An object was real, solid, and unchanging, except according to understood rules. We were living in a world of solidity and reality, and color as a real quality of objects had never been questioned. Then scientists discovered that color is not a quality of the object but a quality belonging to light. For example, a tree appears to be green only because its leaves absorb all the reds in the light it receives and reflects the greens; those greens change in appearance to the eye as the surrounding atmospheric conditions change, so that color is not unchangeable, as had been thought, but is variable with the position of the sun, with the change in atmospheric conditions, and with the effect of other surrounding colors. Thus, a white spot surrounded by green was found to appear reddish to the eye because of laws of optic nerves. The whole conception of color was changed.

These scientific discoveries in the realm of color were the opening wedges in the cracking up of our conception of the world as solid and real and unalterable. A group of men in France, later to be known as the impressionists, seized upon these new discoveries in light and applied them to painting. In order to catch the constantly changing color effects in nature, they worked only a short time each day on a canvas, only as long as the position of the sun and the atmospheric conditions remained constant. They discovered that shadows, which had up to that time been thought of as black, were in reality, that is, in appearance to the eye, of many colors, mostly blue and lavender. The shadow on the face of a man standing under a tree is green. The artists looked, saw this

PLATE IX

"I Am Throwing Something into the Trash Basket"

A child draws what he feels in his body and what he knows, not what he sees. The picture of someone throwing or reaching to grasp an object will have hands and arms exaggerated in size because the child feels the action of throwing or reaching in his own hands and arms. (From *Creative and Mental Growth* by Viktor Lowenfeld, published by The Macmillan Company, New York.)

"La Goulue" by Toulouse-Lautrec

Line in a drawing is closely allied to the artist's emotional state. It is as indicative of character as handwriting. Toulouse-Lautrec's line is nervous and quick-moving. (Courtesy of the Art Institute of Chicago.)

"Street Scene" by Kirchner

No two artists have the same quality of line. A line may be smooth and flowing or nervous and quavering or harsh and broken. (Collection, The Museum of Modern Art, New York. Gift of Curt Valentin.)

PLATE X

"Pierrot and Arlequin"
by Picasso

Picasso's line is sensitive but calm and assured. So closely is line linked to the nerves and muscles that it may reflect the very heartbeats of the artist. (Courtesy of the Art Institute of Chicago.)

A Degas Drawing

The artist's feelings of excitement or of peace and harmony will flow unconsciously through his brush or pen. (Courtesy of the Metropolitan Museum of Art.)

PLATE XI

"Le Chahut" by Seurat

The painting of Seurat demonstrates that a great artist will produce great art in spite of the handicaps and restrictions imposed upon him. Seurat's painting is great in spite of the impressionist technique. (Courtesy of Albright Art Gallery, Buffalo, New York. Photo, courtesy of The Museum of Modern Art, New York.)

PLATE XII

"On Morse Mountain" by Marin

An American example of modern simplification and organization of picture material. (The Philip L. Goodwin Collection.)

Plate XIII

Cézanne opened new paths of exploration to all the artists who came after him. (Courtesy of the Metropolitan Museum of Art.)

PLATE XIV

"Breakfast" by Juan Gris

In cubist painting the surface of the canvas became more important than the
object portrayed, and the greatest possible richness of texture was the goal.
(Collection, The Museum of Modern Art, New York. Lillie P. Bliss Bequest.)

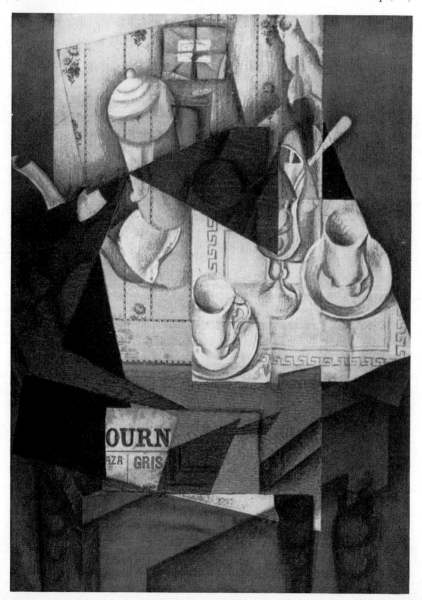

"Ma Jolie" by Picasso

The cubists broke up their material into planes which they pushed to right or left, up or down, to increase the surface tension, for rhythm or balance. The artist insisted on his right to arrange material according to the laws of art and not according to the facts of visual reality. (Collection, The Museum of Modern Art, New York. Lillie P. Bliss Bequest.)

PLATE XV

"The Mocker Mocked" by Klee

Klee is an example of a branch of surrealism using childlike or primitive symbols in a kind of super doodling technique. (Collection, The Museum of Modern Art, New York. Gift of J. B. Neumann.)

"Swifts" by Balla

The Italian futurists explored ways of representing motion. (Collection, The Museum of Modern Art, New York.)

PLATE XVI

and painted it green. They also discovered that pigment when mixed on the palette became dull and muddy because of the impossibility of manufacturing colors as pure as light, but that if those same pigments were put on the canvas as they came from the tube, in small dots or dashes, at a little distance they would be mixed by the eye and in this way retain a much greater brilliance. Therefore, instead of mixing blue and yellow to make a green, the impressionists painstakingly stippled or dotted the colors on the canvas. The results dazzled and amazed gallerygoers, who were accustomed to the dull, muddy tones of the preceding artists—amazed and, strangely enough, outraged them. Since to us now impressionist painting seems rather old-fashioned and far from shocking, it is interesting and enlightening to read what the critics of the day had to say about it.

The experiments of the impressionists were in the realm of technique and science, and impressionism, in the strict sense of the word, has died out today. Only their influence remains. Never again can we be satisfied with color as it was used before the impressionists made their experiments. We are accustomed now to a richer fare, and though present-day artists do not use the dot-dash technique, they do use color in a richer, more brilliant way than ever before. They also use it in a freer way. If local color is not invariable, but can be changed by such extrinsic circumstances as reflections and atmospheric conditions, the artist sees no reason why he should not change it to further his artistic ends. If a face can appear green under a green light, why can it not appear green when the artist needs a green to strengthen his color composition? The impressionist school died out because it was pursuing absolute realism, the imitation of the appearance of things. In their interest in light its practitioners lost all feeling of the solidity and reality of the object on which the light falls, and they had no interest in organizing their canvases. They confined themselves too closely to a limited realism, the exact copy of the effects of light, and when that was attained, they came up against a stone wall. There was no further path to follow. Some of these artists, such as Monet, lost themselves and their creative impulse in scientific research; others, Seurat for example (Plate XII), were more flexible and created fine pictures in spite of the restrictions of the technique; but impressionism itself proved to be a dead end.

Nevertheless, without it the new paths might never have been found, for it was Cézanne who first explored these new paths, and it was the impressionists who started Cézanne's thinking along the lines of form and color. Never in the history of art have there been so many diverse lines of experiment, such rapid advances in techniques, such mental activity among artists as in the years since Cézanne began to paint. Most of the modern movements stem directly from him, and experimenters in the others admit that without his work their trends could never have come into being. (See Plate XIII.)

What were these ideas or techniques that caused such a ferment and led to the types of painting that we call "modern art"? The basic principle was a change of accent from nature to the mind of the artist, as reflected in the painting. The conception of painting had become more and more a visual matter, and less and less attention had been paid to the artist's expression and to the work of art as a new creation. Artists and public valued the picture for its relation to life. Cézanne changed the accent from nature to the work of art, and made conscious what had been the unconscious aim of good artists. He was the first of the modern painters who returned to the principles of freedom from the object. The fact that a work of art is a new creation expressing the artist's sensibility had been completely lost sight of. Cézanne refused to copy nature

102

and rearranged the life elements before him in an expressive pattern. This opened the way for the type of painting usually called expressionism, of which more later.

Another new principle that opened other paths of research was Cézanne's use of color as an intrinsic part of form. Instead of creating forms and then coloring them, he made color and form inseparable; the color *was* the form. In order to give the feeling of solidity, weight, and depth that we get from nature, Cézanne broke his forms into planes, which are made to retreat or advance by the use of cold or warm tones. It was this phase of his painting that the cubists seized upon and carried to greater extremes.

In the early twentieth century, almost simultaneously, Fauvism, cubism, and futurism sprang up. Most of the isms of which we shall speak were named and fostered by literary men, not by the artists themselves. Either literary men became interested in and attached themselves to an artistic movement and issued manifestos to explain and codify what the artists were doing, or artists allied themselves with literary groups who were aiming at the same ends in literature that the artists were striving toward in painting. The ground was ready to receive the ideas of Cézanne. There was the beginning of a general reaction against the visual objective painting of the past, and when Cézanne appeared, his ideas were adopted with enthusiasm.

In 1905 a group of young artists exhibited pictures that reflected Cézanne's influence in the expression of the emotion of the artists at the expense of the accustomed realism. These young men were Matisse, Derain, Vlaminck, Braque, and a few others. The public was so bewildered and astonished that they called this group of painters "les Fauves," the wild beasts. The work of these men represented a break with the past and its rules and ideas that art should represent the external appearance of things as we see them in space. It represented a reversal of point of view. The mind and soul of the artist were the source of artistic inspiration now. Color and shapes were combined in such a way as to give a definite suggestive effect, to evoke an emotion similar to that felt by the artist. To this end they took liberties with nature; they distorted and dislocated stable objects for a rhythmic effect. Nevertheless, the objects were recognizable, and the effect on the public was as though the visible world had become intoxicated and was reeling before their eyes. But though this group shocked and awakened the public of that time, they were only a short step from visual realism.

A further step was taken by the cubists. Seizing on Cézanne's use of colored planes to give a three-dimensional feeling to a canvas, the cubists further broke up the plane surfaces of objects and tried to reduce all objects and masses to simple, geometric shapes—spheres, cones, or cubes. Trying to put on canvas the entire surfaces of objects, not only those that could be seen from one position, they painted all the plane surfaces, accenting the breaks between planes, flattening the rounded surfaces, and opening them out like a deck of cards. The next step was to attempt to show the back and top and bottom, as well as the front, and then to show cross sections combined with elevations. This was indirectly an influence of the machine, as it was the use of the kind of projection drawing used in their construction. After the planes were opened out, they were then arbitrarily pushed to right or left, up or down, to control the movement of the eye or to increase the depth or to provide balance and harmony. The cubists were trying for a tight and balanced organization of the entire canvas, for a dynamic tension between the planes.

Interpenetration and transparency were discovered as means in painting. *Interpenetration* is the combination of two forms,

104

one completing the other; for instance, a part of the outline of a table becomes also one side of a mandolin. This ties objects together and gives the effect of a witty brevity. It has often since been used in advertising art, for which its economy of means is useful. *Transparency*, or the X-ray view, was adopted by artists as the result of the discovery of the X-ray photograph; one object continues to be visible behind another.

All of these new means that the cubists grasped and put to the service of art are nonvisual in the old sense of a one-viewpoint reproduction of what one man's eyes see from a given spot. They are based on what we know about objects and what our eyes have seen at different times and from different points of view. Texture became of more importance. The surface of the canvas having become more important than the object portrayed, the greatest variety and richness possible was aimed at, and especially through the use of a variety of materials. Fragments of newspaper, sandpaper, glue and sand, cloth, wood, and anything else with interesting surfaces were fastened to the canvas. Color, however, was kept to a dull, uninteresting tonality of grays and browns. (See Plate XIV.)

Cubism passed through two major phases, which have been called the *analytic* and the *synthetic*. The first phase, analytic cubism, consisted, as the word *analytic* indicates, of the separation and simplification of the parts of objects. Planes which in the object are subtly modeled and indefinite were flattened; the edges were sharply defined; all the parts were separated by definite boundaries and reduced to their simplest geometric shape. These planes were then considered as separate unities and pushed out of their natural places, to right or left, up or down, in order to increase the tension between them or to produce an effect of rhythm and balance.

In synthetic cubism the unseen parts of objects were added

to the picture. The back, top, bottom, cross section, and any other information the artist had about the object were synthesized and portrayed. These various views and parts were arranged in a more or less arbitrary way, according to a judgment of value; that is, the aspects of the object that the artist considered most useful to his purpose were placed in the most important part of the composition, regardless of their actual relationship. The artist insisted on his right to arrange material according to the laws of art and not according to the facts of visual reality. (See Plate XV.)

Cubism opened several new paths of exploration to modern artists, but cubism itself, as a school or movement, died out, partly because the restrictions imposed by its methods were too confining to the creative artist. But it left behind it a rich inheritance of possibilities that today's artists are exploring and of techniques that are still in use.

The futurists were a group in Italy who also began experimenting with new techniques at the beginning of this century. They were interested in movement. They realized that we live in a dynamic world, that nothing is static, and that only through movement can balance be maintained and life exist. They were also fascinated by machinery, by its smooth mechanical movements and its functional qualities, and they considered the machine the true representation of our times. They considered movement in itself typical of our civilization and paid a kind of worship to the machine as the embodiment of movement at its most efficient peak. It was their aim to show not only human beings and animals in motion, but also automobiles and airplanes and other mechanical contrivances. They experimented with many methods, but the commonest device for dealing with this problem of movement was to portray the same object—or person—over and over again on the same canvas in different aspects of a continuous motion. (See Plate XVI.) We have since often seen this in photography, in such examples as a series of photographs of a man running, each photograph overlapping the last, so that as the eye moves through the series, we see the different movements that combine to give an idea of the direction and the motions of body involved. Futurism as a school very soon died out. In its way it was as realistic as any of the antiquated approaches to art that it was trying to replace. Its aim was an exact copy of a body in motion, and the movie camera and the stroboscopic photo can do that better for us. In spite of all its experiments and the stream of high-flown philosophical explanatory literature its writers poured out on the subject, the futurist school never really managed to deal successfully with the problem of movement in a painting. A famous example of a combination of the techniques of cubism and futurism is the "Nude Descending a Staircase" by Marcel Duchamp, which caused such a furore at the Armory Show in New York in 1912.

Technological advance inspired artists in the first decade of our century. Its preciseness and economy of means appealed. It seemed the only real advance in the social life of our time. Its real order and economy of purpose seemed man's hope for the future. And so, taking over this viewpoint from the futurists, the machine school arose and continues at the present time. The principles of the construction of machines are used in this art, as well as the outside forms of the machines. The meagerness of emotion aroused by this type of art stems from the confusion of technique and art. The accent is on technique and not, where it belongs, on the emotional content of the picture.

All over Europe new ideas and new points of view were boiling up. The discoveries by the scientists and the new theses of philosophers were taken up by the literary men and shared by the artists. Groups of painters banded together in Russia, in Germany, in Italy and experimented with new forms and new techniques. Passionate discussions of theories on art were held wherever two artists got together. There was a search for a more profound reality than the mere visible appearance of things and for new and more powerful ways of expressing this reality. About 1907 the influence of Negro sculpture spread like wildfire among European artists. They saw in those crudely powerful carvings an appeal to the primitive instincts of our deeper natures, an expression of genuine, though brutal, sensation. These primitive works seemed to break through the layer of the stale, traditional ways of looking at art, through the veneer of the intellectual approach, and come into contact with the deep, rich sources of human emotion. The lesson the artists drew from this was that simple, elementary forms inspired by an intense spiritual emotion were at the basis of a living, creative art.

Then came the First World War and after it a feeling of general disgust and despair. Life seemed meaningless, cruel, and stupid, and as a reaction against it, the Dadaists painted their provocative and meaningless pictures. "Destroy by nonsense" was their motto, since everything is nonsense and meaningless. Every value had seemed to break down under the impact of war; religion was hypocritical and futile; science had led only to the production of better means of killing; literature had proved to be only a means of propaganda. All around them these men could see only the debris of moral ruin, and their urge was to clear the ground, to get rid of everything indiscriminately. Einstein's theories of the universe had shaken the ideas held by men for thousands of years, and these, combined with the discovery of the atom, and the scientific corollary that this world around us and everything in it is not solid and tangible but a mass of electrical discharges, had started to have an influence on the thought of writers and artists even before the war. The work of Freud had reorganized our conception of the human mind. The form that Dada took was partly the result of these feelings of instability and disorientation. It was purely a destructive movement and as such was bound to be short-lived.

Other young artists and writers were searching for new, constructive paths. Since their confidence in the rational mind of man and the experience of our senses had been shaken, they fell back upon the subconscious mind, the source of our energy, the basis of our emotion and desires. This movement was started by French writers, who, clearing their minds of all conscious thought and in a passive state, wrote whatever nonsense came into their heads. The writers found that the words, although meaningless, carried with them an evocation of emotion, and that words which had become stereotyped and banal in their usual context became fresh and powerful when grouped in a new way. Because they were seeking for a reality truer and more vital than the illusions of our senses and the commonplaces of the world of everyday, they called themselves *sur-* or *above*-realists. They rejected all the old forms of our culture that are based on reason, and they held in contempt all clear and rational intelligence. In this respect they were an outgrowth and continuation of Dada, with a constructive element added, that they did believe in and rely on the subconscious, the primitive in man. They trusted in and glorified all the underlying urges and cravings that our egos reject and control and that our consciences condemn.

Although surrealism was in the beginning a purely literary movement, it was not long before the artists got into it and eventually took it over. It proved to be more adapted to the techniques of painting than to those of writing, and it was through the painters that the movement spread and became known throughout the world. The literary surrealists fell into internal dissension, a battle of theories, and eventually split into several groups. Meanwhile, the painters, reinforced by émigrés from Nazi Germany, formulated a definite and more constructive platform for surrealism. Their theory was this: As children we are able, with the aid of any commonplace object (an old shoe box, a heap of sand), to enter into a satisfying, enchanting, magic world composed of a fusion of imagination with the world of reality. This power we lose as we grow older and intelligence takes command. Eventually our lives become dull routine and utter boredom. By destroying the habits of intelligent thought and freeing the imagination, we can again acquire that fusion of the imagination with the cosmos and recapture the fresh magic of our childhood sensations. This did not mean that we must return to infantilism, but that we must first destroy our habit-patterns of thought, return to the point at which they began to form a crust over our free imaginative activities, and reeducate them. The destruction of our thought habits is an essential tenet of surrealism, and it is brought about by a systematic use of humor in relation to everything the intelligent mind has been taught to hold as true or respectable. The ultimate aim is the union of man with the universe, the mystic illumination that comes when our essence combines with the essence of the cosmos.

There are two main tendencies in surrealistic painting. There is the school, of which Salvador Dali is the best-known proponent, in which the images that rise from the subconscious in dreams are used as picture material, and homage is paid to Freud and psychoanalysis. The difference between this school of surrealist art and other types of art is simply that the original material of the painter is not before him at the moment. The material is derived from former experiences and seen objects transmuted and reassembled during a long period of submergence in the subconscious. This type of surrealism gains greater impact on the spectator if the technique employed is extremely realistic. A photographic realism is usually used, and by contrast with the fantasy of the subject material it gives us a duality that shocks and surprises. Dali's technique is an example. It is necessary, in order to make us believe in this dream world, to clothe the motives employed in a fabric of concrete realism. The danger of this kind of painting is that it may become too personal, that the images employed may be based on individual experiences which have meaning only to the artist or to the few. If the dream images are universal in scope, if they are the dreams of all of us, surrealist art may be a catharsis, a release for hidden tensions and fears. It may also be good or even great art, not because it is an art based on dreams, but because the man who employs this technique is an artist.

Of the other trend in surrealism Klee is the best example. This school or subgroup uses the symbols of children and of primitive peoples as its material, in combinations and arrangements dictated by the subconscious by means of an automatic-writing technique. The artists consciously use naive, simplified art signs borrowed entire from or influenced by the type of symbol making used by people in an immature stage of development. They choose these symbols, rather than more sophisticated and more personal ones, because they feel that they are more universal and touch us on a level of consciousness that has been formed in us all at an early stage and overlaid by later experiences. To touch us on this level is to arouse the fresh sensations of childhood. The automatic-writing technique by which these symbols are united and composed also comes from depths below the conscious level. It is super doodling; that is, the conscious mind abdicates or

111

is occupied elsewhere, and the hand moves under the influence of the subconscious mind. The conscious mind resumes control only to check and correct the finished product.

In this type of surrealism the technique as well as the material provides surprises and shocks. Shock is a necessary ingredient of surrealism. It is through shock that the artists hope to break up our thought habits and penetrate through the crust of our daily reactions, which have become stereotyped and automatic, to the depths of our primitive natures, whence the richest responses to art spring. Although surrealism was launched as a modern and novel approach to painting and literature by a group of French writers between the two world wars, we see that in reality only the *word* surrealism is new; the attitude and technique have always existed in art as a natural expression of man's dreams and fears. Dali and Klee are only the latest exponents of timeless art thought patterns which produced, among others, Bosch and Breughel in painting and Rabelais in literature. (See Plate XVII.)

The spirit of experiment was strong in Germany up to the advent of Hitler and in Russia until modern art was declared, oddly enough, reactionary. In Holland a very pure (that is, a very abstracted) art was developed, an art of hard, simple, geometrical forms. Here the modern movement was called de Stijl and neoplasticism. The aim of this Dutch school of art was restriction with equilibrium, the most economical means to suggest a sense of balance in space. The artists worked on a perfect measured relationship, simplifying and analyzing the relationships of highly simplified forms on flat surfaces. To them the problem of breaking up the space became a mathematical or purely intellectual one quite divorced from the problems of aesthetics. They rejected all the sensuous elements in art and were left with a dry and arid formula.

Mondrian went so far into abstraction that he restricted his forms to arrangements of rectangles, vertical and horizontal, and his colors to the primary colors, red, blue, and yellow. In spite of these extreme limitations that he imposed upon himself, he was able to express a refinement of sensibility and perception, proving again that any technique in the hands of an artist can produce a work of art. (See Plate XVIII.) The work of the Dutch artists has had a great influence on architecture and on advertising art in which the clean, simple, abstract shape can be used to advantage.

Expressionism was the label attached to the new movement in Germany in the early years of this century. An exhibition of the work of Braque, Picasso, and Derain held in Germany in 1910 inspired the artists there to experiment along new lines. Kandinsky, a Russian artist working in Germany, pushed the abstraction of forms even farther than had the French artists (Plate XVIII). He and the other artists who banded together under the name of the Blue Riders painted some completely abstract pictures, in which no natural object could be recognized, but in which the forms and colors had a value in themselves as agents for arousing or communicating emotion. The difference between the German group, the expressionists, and the other groups working in the new art fields in Europe was the accent placed by the Germans on emotional content. In their work there was less of a mathematical or scientific approach, less insistence on techniques, and more insistence on freedom and expression of feeling and idea. They worked in a state of strong inner tension and thought of their painting in terms of music. In the best of American and European painting today the new techniques that the French artists have discovered and explored are combined with the rich, emotional qualities and spontaneous excitements of the German painters.

The rest of the isms that we have mentioned, vorticism, suprematism, constructivism, etc., were all names applied to local groups working along lines more or less similar to those we have briefly analyzed. In some cases the accent was on new technical discoveries, in some cases on greater freedom of expression, more direct, simple ways of communicating emotion. Much of this experimental work is almost valueless from an aesthetic point of view, but all of it has been useful in broadening the possibilities of art.

Let us give a brief and very generalized survey of the ways in which visual objects, the material of art, are modified in what we call "modern art." They may be simplified. *Simplification* is another word for *abstraction*, perhaps the most outstanding characteristic of modern art. This simplification may be based on mathematical or geometrical rules; the artist seeks in nature for underlying geometrical forms and eliminates everything extraneous to these forms. Or the simplification may consist in seeking the most universally characteristic aspect of the natural object and eliminating all accidental or personal aspects. The danger of the first type of simplification is that, if pushed to a logical extreme, it produces barren, uninteresting, cold results, which involve our minds but not our emotions. Good results can be obtained by this method, as by all other methods, when it is used by an artist who finds it a natural means of expression and who has something to express.

The second means used by artists in what we call "modern art" is *symbolism*. This, as we have seen, is also far from being a modern technique; it is found throughout the history of art. Symbolism is still being used in both the forms of which we have already spoken—that is, a symbol in the sense of a hieroglyphic, a characteristic part standing for the whole, and in the sense of a concrete object standing, by association, for

114

an abstract idea. The dangers of the first type of symbolism are few. We all recognize a characteristic part and can imply the whole. The weakness of the second type of symbolism is that the associations may not be universal. I may not understand the symbolism involved by association in the mind of a Chinese between a dragon and certain religious myths and ideas; he may not understand the symbolism of a fish, or even a cross, as connected in our minds with the whole fabric of Christianity. However, this type of symbolism is of what we may consider secondary value in a painting. If the painting is a fine one, with all the qualities of greatness, we can enjoy it even without understanding the symbolic significance.

The third method employed in modern art is *exaggeration*. Just as the artist eliminates the nonessentials of his material, so he accents the essentials. This exaggeration may be applied either to the form, in which case it is purely visual, or to the emotional factors. For instance, Cézanne exaggerated the plane surfaces of objects in order to accent the effect of solidity that he felt in nature and that had never been adequately expressed on a two-dimensional surface. For an exaggeration of the emotional qualities we may cite Rouault, George Grosz, and Soutine, who are continuing the tradition of Daumier, Hals, and Goya. (See Plate XIX.)

Simplification, exaggeration, symbolism—we have seen these methods used throughout history. Nonrepresentational art, as many artists working today prefer to call their painting, is an old story. We find it in Scandinavian art centuries ago, in Indian art in America, among the Aztecs and Mayans, in the decorative art of the Near East. The sculpture of the Easter Islanders of undetermined age compares well in nonrepresentational quality with the art of Henry Moore, disciple of the "modern." (See Plate XX.)

The first of these general methods, abstraction, is the quality

115

that comes to the minds of most of us when we think of modern art. This tradition of abstraction, which has been strong in most of the great periods of art, has been revived by modern artists and has been pushed farther than had ever before been done in easel painting. Complete abstraction, the reduction of natural objects to simplified geometrical form, has always been common in the so-called "decorative arts," in pottery, textiles, and, in fact, all the arts in which the surface to be covered was considered important in itself and the design an embellishment of that surface. That is the attitude held today by many easel painters, and it developed as a necessary reaction to the dangerous storytelling view that was generally held in the nineteenth century and is still quite common today.

Another contribution to art made by the researches of the last fifty years is the renewed insistence on the importance of the work of art in contradistinction to the nature object; that is to say that in a work of art two elements only are of importance: what the artist has to say, and how he says it. What inspired him to say it is of no importance. These general attitudes have been held by artists of all times and countries but have been most clearly formulated and generally understood recently.

In addition to the change in general attitude and the revival of techniques that had been more or less forgotten or relegated to the decorative arts and handicrafts, the modern movement has made two other contributions to the stream of art. There has been new material available. The new material consists of things seen through mechanical eyes more delicate and powerful than our own, the objects seen under microscopes and telescopes and recorded by the camera. These are things never seen by man before our time. By slowing down the movie camera, we can see objects in action too fast for

116

the human eye to perceive. Machines, too, are new material for art, visual objects that are now familiar to all and were unknown to artists of other epochs. The machine, with its clean, functional lines and moving, interrelated parts, is the motive of such artists as Léger, as well as the basis for their theories and techniques.

New attitudes or a revival and accentuation of old attitudes that had been forgotten by artists of the main stream and that survived only in periphery art, in the art of primitive people, and new material made available to the artist through modern inventions, called for new ways of expressing these attitudes and handling this material. Many experiments have been and are being made in techniques. Many of these experiments are abortive and lead nowhere, but many pass into the general language of art. For example, since Cézanne's time most artists consider color as a part of form and not as an end in itself. Formerly color perspective was used to give depth to a canvas. We orient ourselves in space by our knowledge of value changes and color changes in distances. Modern artists eliminate this kind of perspective and assign to values the definite role of organizing space on the picture plane. Exaggeration of color and value contrast gives a greater sense of space. Both condensed and stretched scales of color and value are used. Instead of using color and light and shade as seen from one point, the eye, artists now use them as seen from many points, because actually in life light is moving and transitory. Shifting the direction of light on the canvas and indicating multiple points of source for the light give the effect of life and movement. Sometimes color is used structurally; a surface is a color plane and not a colored plane.

Modern artists are extremely concerned with space. Man's attitude toward the world is bound up with his feeling for space. Form is inconceivable apart from space, and form is

117

the body and bones of art. In child art and primitive art the problem of space is handled on the basis of value judgments; the relationships of objects in space are determined by the emotional or aesthetic importance of the object to the artist. The most important objects are largest, whether they are near or far. There is no overlapping; near objects do not conceal objects that would to our eyes be behind them. In the time of the Renaissance the laws of perspective were worked out to present spatial relationships as seen from one point of view by one pair of eyes. This is the way things look to us and to a camera. Parallel lines appear to approach each other until they meet at a vanishing point on the horizon. The exuberant Renaissance artists were delighted with this discovery and played with it for its own sake, often to the disadvantage of the aesthetic effect of the picture. They would paint long vistas of arched columns, between which the spectator was invited to walk, back, back, back, into the depths of the canvas until he found himself continuing on into infinity with no way out. After the first novelty of the discovery of perspective had worn off, artists realized that a one-point-of-view perspective composition was static and did not give the feeling of movement which we have constantly in life. In spite of our one-view vision of life, objects before us are never static; even if they have no movement in themselves, the slightest motion of our heads changes our view of them and consequently their outline. The next experiment the artists made to correct this dead and static effect was to use multiple viewpoints combined with perspective. The receding lines would meet at two or more vanishing points. But still the vision was conceived from the viewpoint of man's eyes, and the basic structure of composition was vertical and horizontal —horizontal as the earth is, vertical as a man standing on the earth.

118

Now, in modern art, man is trying to deal with space in new ways. Einstein and the physicists have given us new conceptions of space. Aerial and microphotography have shown us the possibility of viewpoints other than from one man's eyes. Perspective as a means of describing our relation to space has been largely abandoned and with it the single or multiple viewpoint. Space is now defined by the interrelationship of colored forms with each other and the spectator. Color, by means of the advancing and retreating qualities of cold and warm tones, plays a large part in the spatial orientation. When the imaginary spectator with his single pair of eyes was abandoned, so was his relationship to the earth, the horizontal and vertical structure. The axis of picture composition was tipped and became a diagonal. A diagonal involves movement; it has a seeming tendency to revolve. Therefore perfect balance became imperative, and we have, in modern art, a composition of delicately balanced movement.

Greater emphasis is placed on surface texture in modern art. Since the early experiments of the cubists in gluing various materials to the canvas to procure a variety of textures unobtainable with paint, our feeling for surface quality has been sharpened, and we demand a greater richness and variety. Though most artists have abandoned the help of glued-on newspapers or sand and depend on the paint itself, there are still a few who use any materials available to enrich their surfaces.

Remembering again that we are talking only about the means and not the spirit of art, let us try to summarize what is truly *modern* in modern art, what is a revival of old techniques that had been more or less abandoned, and what is simply a change in accent or attitude toward already existing conceptions. In the first place, there is quite a mass of new forms for the artist to work with, forms never before beheld

119

by human beings, the shapes made by the earth as seen from miles up in the air, and the shapes of microorganisms. Machines used as the raw material of art and the influence of mechanical drawing of machines, with its cross section and projection, are new. Interpenetration, with one object continuing and completing the mass or outline of another object, and transparency, with one object seen through another, are new techniques that we owe to the invention of the X ray. They are probably a permanent addition to the tools of art because of their usefulness in giving a feeling of unity to a picture. And that is about all we moderns can boast of as having added to the tools and materials of art.

Among the revivals of old techniques is the use of simplified forms, abstraction. The utility and importance of this essential method of art creation had been lost sight of by artists of the main stream, but it had continued to be used by primitive artists such as the Dahomans in their sculpture and by artisans working in the tradition of decorative peasant handicrafts. This is the way art theories are carried on when they are swept out of the main stream. They are kept alive on the level of folk art until the need for them arises again. The use of a no-viewpoint organization is an example. We find it in patterns on textiles and pottery, but its conscious use in easel painting is new. The use of dream or imaginative material is as old as history. We find it in the art of all peoples. It springs from an integral part of the human personality. Good examples of the fantastic-imaginative are found in Mayan art of the second century B.C., but it is found in nearly all arts. The only novelty in this type of painting in our own day is the philosophy that has become attached to it and is an extrinsic and unimportant part of it. Abstraction as a conscious technique may be called a revival, too. It is a technique that has been used by artists of all periods, consciously by

120

some, unconsciously by others, but in the century preceding its revival it had fallen into disuse by easel painters. Only the extreme to which it has been pushed in picture making, as distinct from decorative art, is new. The use of color as an end in itself or as a rhythmic device or as a means of spatial organization is a revival. Color from the fourteenth century to the middle of the nineteenth century was considered an attribute of form, and the local color of an object was invariable. But color was used in the decorative arts and peasant arts during that time in a more dynamic way, and prior to that time had been used as a means to pattern organization and not as a means to realism. This aspect of its use today is a revival.

At the basis of what we call "modern art" is a change of attitude on the part not only of artists but also of mankind in general, a change of which painting is only one manifestation. The world about us has changed more rapidly for us than for any two generations of men who ever lived. Our surroundings, the objects we see, our conditions of living, the pace at which we live, as well as our ideas about the universe, have undergone great changes in a very short time. The fact that this formerly solid world has disintegrated before our eyes into whirling, unstable atoms, and the mobility made possible by inventions for the high-speed transportation of people and ideas have given us all a sense of insecurity and instability. We feel the need of simple, stable principles and comprehensible order. This is basically what modern artists are trying to give us, not a piece cut out of our chaotic world and framed, but a new, unified, orderly world, self-sufficient, simplified, complete, and founded on universal principles.

The invention of the camera forced the artist to survey his position and clarify his objectives. If realism was the objective of art, he was henceforth useless. This clear mapping out of

121

the boundaries of the artist's kingdom has had a beneficial effect on art; it has purified it of many extraneous and fortuitous aims and has given the artist greater freedom within the true range of his legitimate objectives. The change of attitude involved can be described as a greater accent placed on the creative freedom of the artist and the self-sufficiency of the work of art. The life objects that furnished the inspiration for the work of art, being no more than a collection of moving atoms anyway, lose all importance to and connection with the finished work of art, which must be judged entirely on its own merits as a newly created organization. The artist feels free to break up and redistribute the various parts of objects on the basis of their importance to his scheme of composition or to his value judgment, which is a personal, emotional matter.

The goal of the modern artist is clarity, precision, and an economy of means. In order to attain these ends he simplifies by abstraction, reducing complicated forms to their most universal possible version. By this means he hopes to make his order more apparent and easily grasped and to appeal to a larger audience. So far he has been thwarted in the latter aim. We are so steeped in the false tradition that art and realism are synonymous that we do not realize that what is happening in the arts is a simplification which should be, and in reality is, far easier to understand than a chunk of real life. We are simply looking for the wrong things and reading into a simple statement complications of our own making.

There, then, are some of the new tools and revivals of old tools with which the artist is working today. Tools and materials do not make a work of art; that depends on who uses them and what he does with them. In any generation there is only a handful of artists on the genius level, a larger, but still fairly small, group of good artists, and a still larger number of competent artists. Each of these men will find the traditions and techniques most suited to his personal needs of expression, and with them he will produce works of art of a caliber in accord with his capacities. So in modern art we have pictures that are good, some that are bad, and some that are indifferent. If we could say, "It is modern, therefore it is good," it would make things very simple for us. Because we are always trying to make our lives simple, there are a good many people who are making the above blanket judgment. And there are many who totally condemn on the same principle. "If it is modern, it is bad." But all these people are missing the whole value that art can give. Next time you look at a modern painting, ask yourself, "Has this artist succeeded in creating a work of art with the tools that the modern movement has put into his hands?"

6

HOW CAN I LIKE PAINTING?

Now we are ready to talk about the role the spectator plays in the threesome of art. In every complete art experience there are the artist, the work of art, and the spectator. The artist may double as spectator after he has finished his act of creation, and the spectator must double as artist to some degree; that is, he must make an effort to enter into the picture and follow the creative process as well as he is able. Let us repeat the important words: *he must make an effort*. Unfortunately we cannot sit quietly at home and soak up art passively like a sponge. We do not get any art in our homes, with the few rare exceptions of more or less inferior reproductions in magazines. We are dependent on the museums and art galleries for our supply of art and we must go

124

to art. It will not come to us. If we live in small towns that do not have museums or art galleries, we must depend upon books from the public library, and the books with good colored reproductions sometimes cannot be taken home.

Growth in the understanding and appreciation of pictures is a slow process like the growth of the body itself, and, like bodily growth, art growth depends on food. The food of art appreciation is pictures. The more pictures we see, the faster will be our growth. We shall assume that we have a real desire to increase our understanding and enjoyment of pictures, that we want to participate in the pleasure and richness they can bring into our lives, that we sincerely long to break down the mental barriers that keep us from communion with the minds of great artists of all times. A little effort is a small price to pay for a new, enlarged world in which the mind can expand and take delight.

The first step to take is to find a source of material, a museum, a gallery, or the public library. It is preferable to find pictures in color—if not originals, at least good color prints that you can take home. It takes time to see a picture. Good pictures have depths of meaning that can only be arrived at slowly, and we ourselves bring to the contemplation of pictures different states of mind, different degrees of sensibility at different times. George Bernard Shaw says about looking at pictures, "Now the right way to go to work—strange as it may appear—is to look at pictures until you have acquired the power of seeing them. If you look at several thousand good pictures a year, and form some sort of practical judgment about every one of them—were it only that it is not worth troubling over—then at the end of five years or so you will, if you have a wise eye, be able to see what is actually in a picture and not what you think is in it." We shall take it for granted that all of us have a wise eye.

You will probably find that in your community it will be very difficult, if not impossible, to get good color prints that you can borrow to take home, but these usually can be bought for very little. It is essential to have pictures at home if you are going to grow in your understanding of them, and you will have to make up your mind to spend the price of a couple of movies on color prints now and then. As you advance in your appreciation of painting, you will do this more and more gladly, but at first it may come hard. We Americans have a block in our minds against buying pictures. We think that only the rich collector buys pictures, and we do not realize that the money we spend in one evening in a night club would buy an original painting that would give us pleasure for life. Fairly good prints can be bought for as little as a couple of dollars, and the original work of young artists who are not yet well known can be picked up for the price of a bottle of good wine or a pair of shoes. Even the paintings of well-known artists can often be bought cheaply or on time payments if you go direct to the artist. If the American public would get the picture-buying habit, the artist could afford to sell his work very cheaply. The price must now be maintained because he can only sell two or three pictures a year. Occasionally certain artists, following the theory that the reason the public does not buy more pictures is that the prices are high, have marked their pictures down to a minimum price within the average budget. Strangely enough, the result has always been the opposite of what they expected; the few people who had been buying their work stopped buying it and no new customers appeared. The reaction of the public was that if it was cheap, it could not be good. Price and quality are linked in the American mind. After we have learned to know a good picture when we see one, we shall not be fooled by prices. We will buy good pictures wherever we find them

126

and at any price, and if we buy enough of them, the artist can afford to sell them cheaply and will be better off than he is now.

We must make up our minds that we are going to buy pictures up to the limit of our financial capacity. We will start with prints, because we are not yet sure enough of ourselves to invest any considerable sum. And even before we start buying prints, we will get books from the library with color reproductions if possible, if not, with black and whites.

Now is the time to take stock of yourself and your motives. You are starting out on an expedition to find the pictures you want to live with and study for the next few weeks. There are thousands of pictures to choose from, the accumulated wealth of the whole world. How are you going to decide which ones to choose? Are you going to look at the artist's name and choose the ones that the high-school art teacher or the professor in the art-history class in college told you were good? Or have you a theory that American art is for Americans and will you choose pictures from the "American school"? Or will you decide to play it safe and choose pictures that everybody knows are good?

The very first step in an art education is the decision that you are not going to play it safe. You are going to take risks, you are going to make mistakes, you are not going to acquire a superficial culture that will impress the Joneses. You are launching on an adventure by yourself and for yourself; you cannot take with you the art teacher or the Joneses. When you go to find your pictures, go alone, not only physically alone, but also mentally—do not take the art teacher with you or the Joneses even though they are only in your mind. Turn them out.

When you are at the print shop or the library and are looking at the pictures to make your choice, cover the artist's name and look only at the picture. You are going to make the very difficult experiment of discovering what you really like. Would you have the courage to say to yourself, "I don't like this picture," if it were signed Leonardo da Vinci or Van Gogh? Maybe you do not really like Leonardo da Vinci, and maybe you have never really seen a Leonardo—I mean *really* seen one, with your "wise eye." The chances are that you have seen the name, Leonardo da Vinci, ticketed the picture in your mental filing cabinet as "good," and looked no farther. Now you are leaving all labels and charts behind. If you don't like Leonardo, why you don't, that's all. Maybe you just have not the Leonardo personality, but you may strike up a friendship with Botticelli or Fra Angelico.

If you are really honest with yourself in this experiment, you may find out a good many things about yourself that you did not know before. But you must be honest in choosing your picture. You must honestly answer this question and no other, "Do I really feel an emotion when I look at this picture?" On this basis you select two or four or six pictures and you carry them home with you. Perhaps you find that you have chosen pictures from different countries and different periods, a Japanese print, a Persian miniature, an Italian Renaissance work, a Flemish genre picture, a French modern painting. In the first chapter of this book we likened types of painting to rivers and said that all artists painting today were the end point or final wave on these art streams. You will probably find that all the pictures you have chosen belong to a single one of these streams, though they may be chosen from different periods. Most of us have a tendency to like one type of painting, and there is more similarity between a realistic artist painting today and a realistic artist of the seventeenth century than between an abstract artist and a realistic artist living at the same time. Matisse, for instance,

128

is more closely allied in temperament to a sixth-century Persian artist than he is to a Miro or a Rouault. (See Plates XXI and II.)

If you are a real novice in art, you are likely to choose the more realistic or storytelling types of art. This is nothing to be ashamed of; realistic art can be good art, as we know. It seems to a beginner easier to understand than the more abstract pictures, but this is a fallacy. Realistic art is more difficult to understand. It is farther from our natural basic ways of art expression, and it throws us off the track of our real art experience and understanding by arousing irrelevant associations. If we are not careful, we find ourselves right back again in our own lives and personalities, instead of losing ourselves in the picture. But we must be on our guard against that with all pictures.

Let us say that you have chosen four more or less realistic paintings. When you get them home, you pin them up somewhere on the wall where you can see them many times a day as you go about your affairs. You can see them when you are in many moods and states of mind, you notice them suddenly with a shock of pleasure and surprise, you glance up from your book and there they are in a new and different light.

After a few days, when the pictures have become a part of your life, you take one down and prop it up on a chair. You then draw up another chair facing this picture, which you think you already know pretty well. The first step is to empty your mind of everything but the picture. You must not think of the pudding you are going to make for dinner or the stenographer at the office who has to be fired. You must just sit there passively, receptively, and look at the picture. Do this for as long as you can concentrate on the picture, and when your mind begins to wander away from it, you must start your catechism.

Ask yourself first, "Did this picture, even for a minute, put me in a state of ecstasy so that I completely forgot myself and my affairs?" If you can answer "yes" to this question, you are very lucky. You are the ecstatic type of spectator, the kind of person who is able to get the best that art has to offer. If you cannot answer in the affirmative, it may simply be that your receptive capacities are blocked or warped, and it will be your job to cultivate and open them up. These moments of ecstasy are never of long duration, but their results in the human personality are lasting. If you have had your moment of ecstasy you have, for the time being, lost your ego, your sense of being you; you have identified yourself completely with the picture. "One becomes that which he is enjoying." * This experience is most common in music. We have nearly all at times been so completely absorbed by a great symphony that we have ourselves become the waves of sound, and we have been returned at the end to ourselves with a sense of having been away into a wider, freer world than that of our body with its limitations and of our ego with its needs and demands.

If, however, your answer to this first question is negative, you must then ask yourself this: "Am I a participator in this work of art?" Now a participator does not lose his identity; he is there playing a part in the situation in person. A typical participator reaction is to feel or imagine oneself walking under the painted trees or enjoying the painted garden as one would enjoy a real one. The participator would like to know, to be actually acquainted with, the painted person. He enters into scenes of action and becomes one of the actors. Sometimes this type of spectator even identifies not only the content of the picture, but also the actual canvas and frame with his own personality and utilitarian life. He says, "I should

* Muller Frienfels, *Psychologie der Kunst.*

like to own that picture," or "I couldn't live with that picture," because it would or would not look well over *his* mantelpiece or on *his* wall. His sense of his own ego and its needs is constantly active.

This type of reaction to pictures is the most common. The ego is strong in man and is plotting and planning away as to how it can use all material in the environment and turn it to its own needs. The ego builds a wall around us. It separates us from the man in the street, the middle class, the capitalist —all these are the other fellow. The artist is the other fellow. We stand alone; *we* are unique. Only in certain aspects and on certain occasions are we willing to subordinate the self for an end. We may become a union member and feel a solidarity with other workingmen; we subordinate the self to a good that is eventually a selfish good, for it will benefit us. Only rarely does man sacrifice his individuality for an ultimate good that benefits only others—rarely indeed. But this individuality that is man's pride is also his trap and his limitation. We long at times to escape from this circumscribed selfhood, to feel that we are a part of a larger and more important whole. Through art we can enlarge our experience. The bounds of the ego are pushed back, and for a moment we catch a glimpse of other vistas, other possibilities. There is a strong necessity in man to escape his tyrant ego and to lose himself in something larger and freer, and this escape, which refreshes and renews us, can be achieved even by the most ego-bound with practice.

The third question in your catechism is: "Am I a spectator?" It is obvious that you are a spectator in the sense that you are sitting there looking at this picture. But have you the spectator state of mind? If you have answered "no" to the first question, if you have not been able to lose your identity or consciousness of self in the picture, and if you have been fortunate enough to answer "no" to the second question, if you have succeeded in not losing the picture in your identity, then you must answer yes to the third question. In the ecstatic relationship between picture and spectator only one thing exists, the picture. In the participator relationship only one thing exists, the spectator. In the third relationship there are two things, the picture and the spectator. This is the most fruitful attitude for an advancement in the understanding of art. Ecstasy cannot be long maintained. The ecstatic is soon returned to the world and becomes a spectator, and in this role he analyzes and observes. And we, as spectators, wait and hope for our moments of ecstasy. They will come.

You are not yet through with your self-analysis and ready to start on analysis of the picture itself. Your next question must be, "Am I seeking a copy of nature in this picture?" Are you consciously or unconsciously judging this work of art by its photo likeness to life objects? Do you want it to deceive you into mistaking it for life? Here it would be well to remind yourself that if it had been the artist's intention to deceive you in this way, he could have done so. Many artists have the technical ability to paint an object so realistically that you would feel you could take hold of it and lift it off the canvas. If realism had been the ideal and aim of artists, sculptors would have made colored statues that would have been exact copies of human beings. When realism arrives at that point, it becomes revolting to us; waxworks, for example, are certainly the ultimate in realism. Art must be like and unlike nature. It must be like enough to give us the key to its meaning and unlike enough to give us a new experience. Artists try to reproduce reality, but a higher reality, and reality is not the same as realism.

Now ask yourself this: "Do I expect this picture to influence my character or actions?" This expectation can take many

132

forms. You should check yourself on all of them. Do you ask this picture to teach you a religious lesson or a moral lesson, or to expound a political or social truth? The value of art cannot be judged by such standards; art does not work in those ways. The influence of art on our conduct, and through that on the political and social environment, is indirect. By making each individual a richer, more understanding person, art does influence our life of action, but the moment art tries to influence conduct directly through moral precept, it loses its true value. Such lessons are better taught through other media.

Art certainly justifies its existence without demanding that it also serve the utilitarian end of improving our morals. Our Puritan ancestors have left us the heritage of a tradition which demands that everything must have a moral or practical use. Some of us have replaced the word *moral* with the word *political*, but the meaning is the same. In politics instead of trying to improve our own conduct we are trying to improve the conduct of society for the common good, a practical good. This is all very well, very well indeed, but we must leave all such considerations behind when we look at pictures. We must let art do us good in its own way; we must let it strengthen and enrich us, broaden our understanding, and refresh our spirits. Then we can go forth and act with greater insight and sensitivity in the world of morals and politics. We must distinguish between what is true and what is false in ethics and morals. True ethics teaches us that all free, creative acts that tend to the growth and happiness of individuals are good. False morality consists in conformity to law, convention, and custom. By this definition art is truly ethical. "To express life implies a certain mastery over it, a power of detachment, reflection, which are fundamentally ethical . . . that we should know life sympathetically is of

133

practical importance," says De Witt Parker. An understanding of life as a whole leads to greater freedom and wisdom in our choices and activities of daily life, a better adaptation to our human environment. Art provides an insight into the whole of life. Art transforms our background of values; it becomes part of our nature and so molds our minds that our every action is influenced by it.

"Do I consider this picture as mere make-believe with no real value?" Your answer to this question will probably be "no." The very fact that you have gone to the trouble of finding the picture and bringing it home and that you are now seated before it spending time looking at it instead of reading a good book or listening to the radio proves that you believe art has some value in itself. But the "mere" attitude toward art is common. Art is a "mere" copy of nature or a "mere" pastime. This view is reflected by the attitude of parents that art is not a profession for a man, and by the public's attitude that artists are irresponsible children.

Ask yourself next, "Am I setting my own limitations on the artist?" Through years of thought habits we establish patterns which become cages. We lose the free flights of fancy we were capable of as children. It is these limitations in ourselves that art can help to overcome, but only if we are willing to follow the artist in his daring mental processes. We must not insist that the artist do it our way. We must be willing to follow him in *his* way of creative thinking and feeling. Art may involve everything in human life that has emotional value. Although as human beings we have many fundamental qualities, a common heritage, fortunately there is an almost endless variety in our humanity. How dull and uninteresting life would be if we were all alike! And yet there seems to be an urge in human nature to force everyone and everything into the familiar pattern of the self, to fear any new and unfamiliar object or experience.

The happenings of the last years point out clearly how dangerous this fear can become. We have seen not only that it diminishes and circumscribes the individual, but also that such an individual, if given power, can turn his fear against a race of people who are different from himself and exterminate them. Dislike of the novel and a standard of judgment based on self as a criterion, while not usually so dangerous to oneself and others, always set boundaries to growth and enjoyment. Therefore it is important to bring to any new thing an open mind, reasoning but ready to accept or reject on merit and not on the basis of familiarity. "In imagination, consciousness proceeds as a whole from the fountainhead of disposition; there are no limits of any kind save those of individual capacity and experience." * "No material should be taboo to art; but all should be dissolved in that alembic whose formula is the secret of the imaginative genius." *

"Am I judging this picture on the basis of taste?" Taste is a social or group criterion, imposed on the individual from without. We absorb standards of taste from our families, from our schools, from the country in which we live. These standards are very different in different parts of the world. The Japanese think that we have very bad taste. We may feel that the African natives are lacking in taste. Taste also changes radically with various periods of history. We are far from sharing the taste of a period as close to us in time and culture background as Victorian England or our own United States fifty years ago. A picture painted in good taste by a Victorian Englishman would revolt a Renaissance Italian. There has always been much painting "in good taste," but as taste is

* F. B. Tichenor, *Textbook of Psychology*, The Macmillan Company.

135

constantly in a state of change, these tasteful pictures are discarded with the clothes of the period. We must distinguish between painting that is simply in good taste (to our present, impermanent way of thinking) and painting of eternal value.

It is taste that dictates fashion, and there are fashions in pictures just as there are in anything we surround ourselves with. Painting of the American scene became a fashion in art recently. Any painting was good if it portrayed a scene on a Midwestern farm with tractors and silos, or a scene of a lynching in the South, or a factory chimney or machine part. In early-nineteenth-century Europe the fashion was scenes from Greek or Roman mythology. The museums were crammed full of them. Where are they now? The moral is: Beware of taste and fashion in art. Remember that taste is a superficial, social, externally dictated, changeable thing, which varies from period to period, almost from day to day. Man expresses even the temporary and superficial through art, for he expresses himself and sees his mind reflected in art. In periods of bad taste, when man is shallow, art will reflect this, and the bad art of the period will be crowned with laurel and hung in museums. But even at the worst periods there are good artists working away unknown and ignored. Let us learn to understand and stimulate the good art of our own period.

Another question in your catechism is, "Do I expect one art to do for me what another could do better?" We often expect painting to do the work of literature and tell or imply a story. We confuse meaning with a story meaning. The meaning of a painting cannot be expressed in words. We might say that anything about a painting that can be expressed in words is extraneous to the real meaning. A painting expresses an attitude and an emotion toward life. Try to express in words your feeling at some deep emotional moment of your life, and you will realize that unless the person to whom you

136

are speaking has had a similar emotional experience, he will not understand. There have been great storytelling pictures. In fact, nearly every rule one can lay down for art has been broken by some great artist at some time. But a storytelling element in a picture, instead of adding to the value of the picture, simply presents a handicap for the artist in succeeding in his true function. When people could not read, painting assumed the duty of educating the public by means of stories, but as this is no longer necessary, we should sharply separate in our minds the functions of painting and literature and rejoice in the fact that we can now have them pure. The reason that storytelling detracts from the true function of art is that a story implies a beginning, a continuation, and an end. A story is a connected series of happenings, and a painting can give us only a part of these events. Our imagination must continue the work and finish the story. This takes us out of the picture and back to ourselves, to our own personal mind. Anything that throws us back to ourselves, anything that allows us to leave the world of the picture detracts from its function of giving us a new and complete experience in a unified whole. It destroys the unity of the painting and the unity of our experience with it.

To go on with your self-examination, "Do I like this picture because it is familiar? Because it is new?" We have already said that if a picture gives you no surprise, if it is simply a repetition of familiar things and thoughts, it has no value for you. Its truth should first shock you and only then should you say, "That is true. I have always felt that but never realized it." Or it may present a truth, in the sense of a true emotion, that you have never even felt before but the validity of which is apparent to you by your reaction to it. Many people are afraid of unfamiliar experiences, even the healthy and stimulating experiences of art. They shrink and close themselves off

137

from the unknown. In order to grow in the appreciation and understanding of art, one must take a risk, one must be willing to undertake adventures of the spirit. The value of art is to communicate feeling, to make new and valuable feelings common, and not to communicate feelings already common.

On the other hand there are people who are attracted to everything that is novel simply because it is new. There are fashions in art as in everything else, and these people will always like the latest thing in painting. If surrealism is the vogue of the moment, they will like only surrealist pictures, but tomorrow they will like only nonrepresentational painting if the fashion in painting has changed. The superficial aspects of painting change with our changing cultures like a suit of clothing, but underneath the body remains the same. Be sure that you are not judging painting by its clothing. We should remind ourselves that, historically speaking, art does not advance, that progression in a line toward a goal of perfection does not take place. The painting of the cave men is as valid, as good, as the painting today. Only the clothing fashions change, the outer forms, and these sometimes change dramatically, but the underlying principles based on the psychological needs of mankind will remain the same as long as mankind endures. The only real advance art makes is in the individual; as he himself grows and changes, his art grows and changes toward a clearer, more complete expression of a deeper and more mature personality. When it ceases to advance, it crystallizes and becomes dead.

Here is the final question you must put to yourself: "Am I willing to abandon my selfhood temporarily and accept that of the artist?" You will probably find that this takes a little practice. The *me* and the *my* have a way of creeping into and coloring our every thought and action. If your ego is not silent, you cannot understand what the artist is trying to say.

138

Just as there are some women, and men, too, for that matter, who talk constantly and thus never find out what others are thinking and feeling, so there are many egos whose demands are so clamorous that they can receive no messages from others. You should try to become completely absorbed by the painting for a little longer period every day.

If you have answered all of the above catechism correctly, you have found that you are not a Puritan (you do not expect art to be a means to a moral end); you are not a Philistine (you do not judge art by its dollar value nor by its sensuous satisfaction); you are not a proletarian (you do not judge art by its propaganda value); you are not a pedant (you do not tabulate names, dates, schools, and other irrelevant, factual data under the impression that you are learning about art). In fact, you have found out a good many negative things about yourself; you know now what you are not, which is a first step in discovering what you are.

After all these negatives we are ready now for the positive question, "What do I expect from this picture?" The answer to this question, like the definitions of art that we have been trying to formulate, should be wide enough to embrace all the manifold forms that art can take and yet narrow enough to eliminate all false or inferior art. Obviously, if you are expecting something from art that it cannot give, you will take away nothing of real value, but only what you yourself have brought to it. You may legitimately expect any of the following things from art: You may expect a new apprehension of truth and reality, a new vision of the world around us, a renewal of the wonder and mystery of life. You may hope for an ecstatic experience, a complete release from self. You can ask that a picture give you a comprehension of the order and relationship of the universe, or of man to the universe.

Now, at the end of this soul-searching catechism, you are

139

purged of all ulterior motives and desires, your ego has retired to some dark corner, you are worthy to commune with great artists. Now let us see whether this picture you have chosen is worthy of you. If you have been looking steadily at it while you were asking yourself the above questions, you have been finding out something about it as well as about yourself. You have also been living with and looking at it for some weeks; it has become as familiar to you as an old friend. But if it is a really good picture, you may be sure that there is still much in it that you have not yet got out. Even very old friends often surprise us by suddenly showing a side of their character that we had never suspected. Although all human beings have deep fundamental traits in common, the outer manifestations of personality are extremely rich and varied, and art, being one of the manifestations of personality, reflects this richness. The greater the picture, the more layers of meaning and significance will be unfolded by long acquaintance. If you find that you are beginning to be bored by this picture, the chances are that you have not chosen it wisely. Perhaps it has no more to give you than a pleasant titillation of the senses; it may be a delightful lyrical "poem" whose appeal charms but does not go below the surface. That kind of picture has value, too, but there is more, so much more, that we can get from art, that we need and have the right to expect.

You now ask a series of questions about the picture, that the picture itself will answer. Some of these questions, you will find, have been answered. The fact that you have taken the trouble to bring home this particular picture, to hang it on your wall and study it, answers the question, "Does this picture give me a genuine emotion?" You must have thought it did when you chose it. So now you will ask: "Does it still give me as much genuine emotion as it did when I first saw it? Does the feeling deepen, or has it worn off? Is it a genuine aesthetic emotion or one of the utilitarian emotions, one of the emotions of our practical life that incite us to action?" If the picture is a good one, it will answer unequivocally; there will be no doubt in your mind.

Now ask: "Does this picture give me something new, a way of looking at things I would never have seen, an idea, an attitude I would never have arrived at myself?" The picture will answer you.

Continue with your examination in less general terms. Is the form this artist has employed historically imitative? Is it simply an old traditional form handed down from the past and reused without being felt? We must distinguish between two kinds of art both of which draw on the forms of the past. One kind truly grows out of principles and definitions that were laid down in an earlier period but were used by a later artist because he understood and felt them. The other is merely an imitative revival. An example of the latter is the Gothic revival in England, where the earlier forms and spirit were totally misunderstood, not felt and not a consequence of a spiritual and social kinship with the original Gothic period. The forms were taken over without sensitivity and externally applied as decoration. If a picture is painted in the style and with the technique of tradition, we must be sure that the artist has made them his own, that they are thoroughly assimilated, and that they are the natural and best way of expressing his unique contribution to art.

Is this form merely decorative, appealing to the senses but not to the deeper layers of our consciousness? That is, does it resemble "applied" art, rhythmic embellishment of a surface with no inner meaning? Is this picture a realistically imitative replica of something already existing, without new life or creative quality? Is the form in this picture dryly practical,

141

worked out on a logical basis in a mathematical formula? In that case it can appeal to our minds only, as the decorative picture can only appeal to our senses.

By this time you should know what the picture is capable of giving you emotionally, and you might try to find out how the artist has managed to convey this emotion, what are the technical means he has employed.

Is this picture a flat pattern or does it rely on depth, on mass, for its effect? How has the artist arrived at balance of form, of color, of line? If you turn the picture upside down, does the balance still feel right? Are the masses balanced by weight or by meaning; that is, do you feel that one side of the canvas is as physically heavy as the other or is the interest balanced?

Now look at the forms employed. Are they flat shapes or three-dimensional masses? If they are flat, the outline is important and should be varied and interesting. Let your eye follow this outline, noting what happens on the way. Note first the quality of the outline itself. Is it arrived at by a line which has a life of its own, or is it simply the edges of two colors that meet? If it is simply the meeting place of two colors, it still has the function of line in that it delimits forms and serves to move the eye, but if an actual line is used, it will have a quality of its own and a part to play in the total effect. As your eye follows around the form, directed either by a line or by the color edges, you will see that variation is introduced by means of curves, straight lines, and arabesques. Curves may be long and gentle or very rounded and abrupt. Straight lines may be short or long and, by changing direction, may form angles. Arabesques are series of curves that reverse to form a flowing, complicated, rhythmic effect. A form outlined entirely by curves or arabesques will be weak and lacking structure; a form bounded entirely by straight lines will be

142

harsh and geometrical; a cunning combination can give us a feeling of delicacy and strength, of poetry and power. Does the boundary of the form in this picture help in what the artist has tried to express; is this combination of curves and straight lines the best means he could use to express his feeling?

Now go back to your starting place and follow the outline again, this time noting color and dark and light. Wherever your eye moves along the outline, there will be two colors meeting, one outside the form and one inside. The variety introduced will be by our old method of contrast and harmony. The hue or spectrum color itself may be contrasted or harmonized; that is, you may have a bright green in the background and a light red in the form. That would be the most violent contrast of hue possible. Or you may have a blue on one side of your outline and a blue-green on the other, making a close harmony of color. Wherever you have a close harmony, you will find that the line as such becomes weaker and the eye passes through it from the form to the background easily. This is rightly called a *passage* and can also be used in the manipulation of lights and darks, or values, as we have called them. So you will see, in moving your eye around the form, that there will be, in places, sharp contrasts of color and value, harmonies of color and value, and passages where the boundary line becomes vague and almost lost and the eye passes freely from the form to the background. You may find it rather difficult at first to force your eye to follow the outline; it may take a little practice. You will find your attention being led across the form and to the center of interest, away into the background and the corners, according to the artist's plan. In most cases he did not intend his outline to hold you continuously all around the form but wanted your eye to move across it and into every part of the canvas.

This might be your next exercise: to try to follow the compositional path the artist has laid out for you. What do you see first and why? Do you see it first because of its placement on the canvas? Because of its greater contrast of color and light and dark? Because of its greater emotional interest? Because of a greater elaboration of line? How does the artist lead you away from and back to the center of interest? Is there something of interest all along the way, even in the most remote corners of the canvas, and are those parts, though interesting in themselves, subordinated to the main interest so that an order and a unity are achieved?

Now analyze the forms themselves. How great a feeling of solidity and depth has the artist imparted? Do you feel that your eye can enter the canvas to the depth of one inch, one foot, or to an indefinite distance? Do you feel that the form has four sides, is completely round, continues around the back where you cannot see it? How heavy does it look? What means has the artist used to impart this feeling of depth? Has he used cold colors to make certain parts retreat (blues, greens, violets), and warm colors to make other parts advance (reds, yellows, oranges)? Has he used inclined planes to suggest retreating sides of forms and lead the eye toward the interior of the picture? Has he used lines that verge toward each other in the illusion of perspective? All these are ways to give a feeling of depth and solidity and the artist may have used one or all of them. Is the form itself a simple mass with only slight modeling, simple indentations, and protuberances like ripples, over which the eye moves smoothly, or is it twisted, contorted, and deeply grooved? In most Venetian Renaissance pictures, in El Greco, and in some moderns, the form is twisted into spirals; the outer plane surfaces and the very core of the form are bent into flamelike, quickly moving shapes. In the work of the Persians and some modern artists

144

like Matisse, the core or axis of the form is static and the surface planes simple and smooth with little feeling of depth. Color is relied on to a large extent for the effect and is laid on in flat and brilliant patches with subtle and strange, or harsh and striking relationships. How has the artist managed space? Has he packed his forms close together and fitted them all tightly into the rectangle of his canvas, or has he left large open spaces in which we have the feeling of being able to move about freely? How far back does his space seem to retreat? There should be a limit to this distance; otherwise the effect will be that of a hole in the picture. Follow the outline of the spaces. Are the shapes pleasing and related to the shapes of the forms? Are the spaces and the forms tied together by means of passages or relationships of color?

If and when your attention begins to stray away from the picture before you, put it back on the wall and resume your interrogation at another time. Learning to appreciate and understand pictures is a good deal like learning anything else; we learn better when our minds are fresh, and after a time we reach a point at which we cannot absorb anything more. Practice will enable us to spend longer and longer periods with pictures, to enter more fully into them, to extract and feel their meaning. The capacity for a real and simple enjoyment of art is in everyone. Sometimes it is atrophied from disuse, sometimes it is warped by a wrong education. Analysis of pictures will help to train our sensibilities to become more receptive. Sensibility itself can be developed just as the muscles of the body can be developed—by use and practice. Most people have stopped growing aesthetically in their early youth. It is difficult and even painful to start growing again, but the rewards are well worth the pain and effort. Appreciation of art is a process of growth, like life itself, and everyone must live for himself—no one can grow for you.

If you find that you have already a deep emotional response to painting, that your sensibilities are acute and do not need developing, you will still profit by analyzing pictures. You will find that an understanding of the principles involved gives you the added pleasure that all intellectual understanding gives. Analysis brings to the attention subtler details and finer rapports which might have escaped notice by an untrained appreciation. Through lack of understanding people expect "to find what cannot be given and therefore are prejudiced against what they might otherwise enjoy." *

By this time we all know what we want from art as distinct from morality or religion or politics or a souvenir to recall past pleasures. We know it gives us something quite different from all these things. We also know that we cannot have at the same time an exact reproduction of natural objects and a new expressive creation of form. We know that nature is uncommunicable and transient, while art is communicable and enduring. In a work of art we communicate through emotion with men living thousands of years ago or yesterday; there are no barriers of time or place. Art touches us on a level of universal humanity where man is fundamental and unchanging. Only a work of art can fix a permanent image of the self, which is the self of all men, so that it becomes a common heritage.

After you have rested your eyes, your mind, and your emotion, have put aside the work of art for a while, you can come back to it with a fresh vision. You can see more readily the means the artist has used to create his work of art. The quality of line, its use in leading the eye or in bounding forms, the way the artist has managed his forms, whether smooth,

* De Witt Parker, *Principles of Aesthetics*, Appleton-Century-Crofts, Inc., 1946.

flat, and static or heavy, deep, and moving, are more apparent. You can quickly grasp his use of color, whether it is handled in a purely lyric manner or helps in the modeling of form, or both. You readily understand his treatment of space and its relation to the forms.

Now you should try to get at the meaning of the picture. First you should remind yourself that art is not the expression of an idea but of an experience, something that the artist has lived and felt deeply. We Americans are so activity-minded that we must keep on reminding ourselves that an experience providing valuable material for art is a purely emotional experience and not an episode nor a continuous action, no matter how dramatic or beautiful that may be. Episodes and activities that unroll in time belong more rightly to the realm of literature. By an experience that the artist has lived we do not mean an adventure or a love affair. We mean simply the emotion aroused by life, either by visual means or through the other senses. Of course it is possible for the artist to translate the emotion aroused in him by an episode in his life if he does not try to tell the story of what happened but to transpose into line and color his feeling about what happened. If the experience is one that is common to all men, the picture will have universal scope; it will be felt and understood by men hundreds of years from now.

Here again we should remind ourselves that subject and meaning are not the same thing. There is a good deal of debate over the question of subject in a picture. One school of thought claims that a truly great picture must have a noble and elevated subject. For instance, to these people a painting of a Crucifixion of Christ must be a greater painting than, let us say, a picture of a pair of shoes. Yet we know that many pictures of the Crucifixion are revoltingly bad and that Van Gogh painted a pair of shoes which arouse in us powerful,

147

pure, and elevated emotions (Plate XXII). That painting will tell some future artist more about the pathos and beauty of our life than any religious picture painted today. But, say these partisans of noble subject matter, given two pictures by the same artist, or two artists of equal caliber, one of a pair of shoes and one of the Crucifixion, the one of the Crucifixion will be of greater value because it portrays a more important and tragic episode. The trouble with this theory is that it takes too temporary and localized an attitude toward art. Even in the world today the people to whom the Christian religion is familiar are in the minority. To a Buddhist or a Hindu a picture of the Crucifixion would carry quite different connotations than it does to us. It might seem, not noble, but the reverse. However, if this picture expresses, not an episode in the life of an individual, Christ, but the feeling of the artist toward religion in general, then it can be understood by all men at all times who are capable of a mystic response. But let us point out that the subject, a man being crucified, will express a mystic feeling of true religion only if the artist has felt it deeply and has succeeded in fusing completely his forms with his feeling and if he has found a perfect means of expressing his emotion. Once again, the feeling of the artist is the important element, not the subject. Some artists may feel about a pair of shoes as deeply as another feels about the Crucifixion, and the quality of two paintings by the same artist, one of shoes and one of the Crucifixion, will depend, not on the subject, but on the artist's feeling about the subject.

A painting, however, can contain many meanings—what are known as *meanings in depth*. But these meanings must be held together by emotion. Take for example Ingres' painting "The Source." (See Plate XXIII.) It is a painting of a young girl holding on her shoulder a jug from which water is flowing. Our first reaction to this picture is what we have called lyric.

148

"The Fall of the Rebel Angels" by Breughel

Surrealism under other names has always existed. (Musées Royaux des Beaux-Arts, Brussels.)

PLATE XVII

"Invention of the Monsters" by Dali

Dali is the latest exponent of a timeless art thought pattern. (Courtesy of the Art Institute of Chicago.)

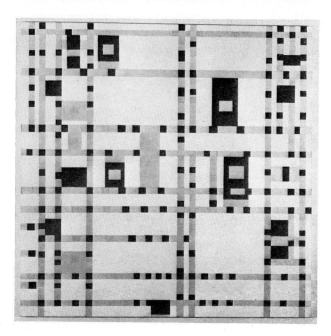

"Broadway Boogie Woogie" by Mondrian

An example of extreme voluntary limitation of means. Mondrian uses only horizontal and perpendicular lines and three colors, yet produces a work of art. (Collection, The Museum of Modern Art, New York.)

Composition VII, Fragment I, 1913, by Kandinsky

Kandinsky produces a sensuous excitement by his use of moving color. Abstraction to the point where no natural object can be distinguished. (Collection, The Museum of Modern Art, New York. Lillie P. Bliss Bequest.)

PLATE XVIII

"Two Sculptors" by Daumier

The painting of Daumier shows an exaggeration of the emotional content of a picture. He also uses simplification of detail and distortion of form. (The Phillips Collection.)

PLATE XIX

Head by Henry Moore

The work of Henry Moore, disciple of the modern, is closely allied in character to that of the unknown sculptors of the Easter Islands. (The Buchholz Gallery.)

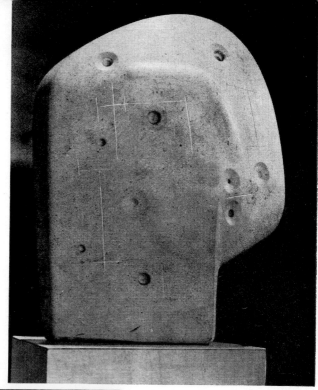

Easter Island Stone Carving

This sculpture might have been produced by a modern artist. The means used are the same. (The American Museum of Natural History.)

PLATE XX

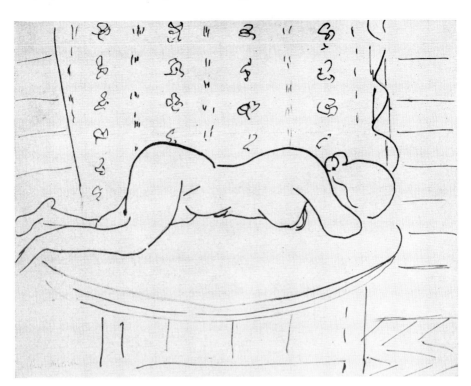

Drawing by Matisse (The Art Institute of Chicago. Alfred Stieglitz Collection.)

Persian Drawing

Persian art maintained its high quality for centuries and still influences artists today. Matisse's flat patterns of color and rhythmic, flowing lines are closer to sixth-century Persian art than to that of today. (Courtesy of the Metropolitan Museum of Art.)

PLATE XXI

PLATE XXII

"Shoes" by Van Gogh

This painting of shoes will tell future generations much about the pathos and beauty of the life of his times. (The Wertheim Collection.)

PLATE XXIII

"The Source" by Ingres

This painting of the classical revival in France is an example of various types of meaning in a picture—sensuous meaning, subject meaning, universal meaning, and meaning in depth. (The Louvre, Paris.)

"Luncheon" by Bonnard

The difference in feeling tone between the Bonnard and the El Greco is marked.
The world of Bonnard is formless, whereas the upward-sweeping and flamelike
forms of El Greco clothe a hard geometric substructure. (Collection, The Museum of Modern Art, New York.)

"The Laocoon" by El Greco

(National Gallery of Art, Washington, D. C., Kress Collection.)

PLATE XXIV

We respond to the low-keyed, subdued color; a tender, poetic feeling tone is established in us by the closely related hues and harmonious values. This feeling tone is reinforced by the smoothly flowing, slow, and gentle lines that define the body and are repeated in the long sweep of water that falls from the jar. We might call this feeling tone the first meaning, the sensuous meaning, because our response to this aspect of the picture is entirely through our senses. Our eyes and nerves and muscles receive the stimuli of the harmonious, flowing lines and colors and respond in themselves. Beyond this sensuous meaning there is another, the subject meaning. This is a painting of a young girl; it may be a particular young girl, but it is also *youth*. The meaning therefore of the subject aspect of the picture manifests the universal quality of youth in the particular young girl. The artist's emotional tenderness toward youth is successfully united to the line, form, and color; the sensuous medium and subject matter are fused so that the one strengthens and reinforces the other. Beyond this subject meaning lies still another meaning in depth. Ingres has felt that young womanhood is the source of the race, that from it flow the future generations just as rivers flow from fresh young springs. Not all pictures have three meanings, but nearly all have two. Some paintings have only the sensuous meaning; they delight us by their color, line, and form, but our response is spontaneous and short-lived, the impact is superficial, and we are likely to tire of them more quickly than of pictures with deeper psychological significance.

Nearly everyone responds to the sensuous meaning in a picture. Some are more sensitive to it than others, but a lack of reaction of greater or less degree to this kind of stimulus is almost as rare as actual physical color-blindness. Our ability to feel, however, can become atrophied and inhibited, and it may take us a little time to get our responses into training again after years of disuse. A good method of conditioning our responses to the purely sensuous side of pictures is to baffle our busybody intelligences by turning our picture upside down. This prevents our minds from interfering with our feelings by asking the wrong questions. Our minds are apt to ask such questions as, "What is happening in this picture?" Nothing is happening in a painting; a painting simply is. This is the difference between asking what a man is doing and what he is. What is happening implies a series of events in time, of which a picture could show a small slice and imply the rest, to be completed by the imagination; but a picture must be complete and timeless. Or our minds may ask, "What lesson does this picture teach?" We have already pointed out that a painting is not a moral or political tract and that its value to the individual and society may be great but must be indirect. Or our minds may insist upon comparing this painting with nature, thereby setting up false and confusing standards of judgment. We know now that no artist intended his picture to be a frame set about a small piece of nature to preserve it like a bug in a jar of alcohol. This picture before us is a newly created thing with laws and standards quite different from those of nature. So when we look at a picture upside down we see it as a pattern of lines, forms, and colors, and our senses react simply and directly, as they do to music. A feeling tone is established throughout our whole physical frame; our nerves and muscles respond, as well as our conscious and subconscious minds.

While you are concentrating on this exercise of the senses, the lyric side of painting, it would be helpful if you could get hold of good color prints of artists who established a widely different feeling tone. A good contrast would be Bonnard compared to El Greco (Plate XXIV). Turn these two artists' work upside down and glance quickly from one to the other. The contrast in feeling response is phenomenal. Bonnard is all soft, glowing, jewellike color with forms that melt into the background like candy on the tongue. Line is almost non-existent in his canvases, even as boundaries for his masses of color. Everything is part of everything else; his fruit, his tables, his people are all made of the same translucent, immaterial stuff. The whole world to Bonnard, from ripe fruit to jewels, is made of a universal material. Now turn to El Greco, and our nerves and muscles respond with an electric shock. Somber colors with great contrasts of lights and darks clothe his violent, rushing forms. Line is very important, both the lines that bound his vigorous forms and the axis lines of the forms themselves. If we put a piece of tracing paper over the picture, lay a ruler along the main line of the picture, and draw them on the paper, we can see that we have a network of lines with complicated architectural relationships, based on triangles of different sizes. So in our upside-down analysis we feel this underlying structure, as hard and solid as a building, and over this structure we feel the swiftly moving forms, darting like upward-sweeping flames.

At this point it might be well to remind ourselves again of the rich rewards in pleasure that can be gained through art. It is difficult and takes time to procure pictures for study. Unfortunately, pictures are not so easily available as books or phonograph records, so we have spent some time in finding a source of supply. Then we have spent a half hour or an hour a day analyzing our pictures, and in busy lives like ours today we want to be sure we are not wasting that time. Doubts begin to assail us. Intelligence is of little or no help in the appreciation of pictures; a real understanding of art is based on instinct. We can understand how we might develop knowledge or intelligence, but we doubt whether instinct can be developed. Perhaps by our analysis we are merely learning a little more about the techniques used by artists, a knowledge which can be pleasurable as the acquisition of any knowledge is pleasurable, but are we actually advancing at all in the real feeling reaction to art? In other words, are we able by the means we are using to develop our art instinct? The answer is probably "no." By these means we are clearing away the accretions of false standards, preconceptions, and inhibitions that prevent our natural instincts from operating.

Emotion is the basis of art; everything else that one finds in a picture is subsidiary to the emotion. Idea, meaning, all the techniques involved are useful only to supplement, express, accentuate the emotion. No art exists without emotion. No matter how intelligent the spectator, no matter how much he knows about all the aspects of art—art history, art technique—if he does not instinctively react emotionally, he knows nothing about art. But the capacity to react emotionally lies dormant in us all, and by constant contact with pictures, by digging away the heaps of wrong facts and misconceptions we have acquired about art, we get down to our simple, real instinct at last. Little by little we shall begin to feel a stirring of our neglected emotional life, and when that happens, the rewards will be so rich that we shall no longer question the value of the time we have spent on this reeducation.

In talking and writing about art, both the artist and the layman must overcome the handicap of a lack of precise terms. There is no established technical vocabulary with an exact meaning for everybody. Writers on aesthetics use the same word with opposite intent very frequently and a great confusion arises. Many people who are seriously seeking to understand art are discouraged by the apparent fact that no two writers on art agree.

One of the greatest points of disagreement, and therefore of confusion of thought in the critic and layman, seems to be the question of subject in a picture. We have discussed meaning and subject and tried to make plain the distinction between them, but let us return to this again and see if we can make it crystal-clear. A meaning implies an intention on the part of the artist to signify something and a response on the part of the observer. The artist's meaning, if not understood by the observer, is no meaning. A sentence in Icelandic is meaningless to a Hindu. We must first learn the language of art in order to understand the artist's meaning. But still we must go further, for this meaning is an emotional meaning. It is not on the plane of our conscious, intellectual minds.

Perhaps this would be made more clear by using the word *significance* for the word *meaning*. Consider the lines, "Go and catch a falling star, Get with child a mandrake root, Tell me where all past years are, Or who cleft the devil's foot." Or consider: "Tiger, tiger, burning bright In the forests of the night." First of all we must understand the English language in order to comprehend the words, but even then the literal meaning of these lines is nonsense. A grammatical analysis does not help us really to understand them. But everyone understands their meaning or significance in the emotional response involved. There should be a better word than meaning or significance to designate the content of emotion that passes from work of art to spectator, but there is not. In music we do not speak of meaning, and there is no confusion between the literary idea of significance and the idea of emotional reaction. However, when we hear very modern music, for which we have no foundation for comprehension, we do say that we do not understand it and understanding implies meaning.

Thus there is the meaning of the line, color, and form, which arouses our lyric emotions, and there is the meaning of the artist's larger intent to communicate a feeling or attitude

153

toward life, and there can be a third or even a fourth meaning, as we have pointed out in the case of Ingres' "The Source." There may even be a storytelling or literary meaning or a symbolic meaning. If these added meanings are thoroughly felt and assimilated by the artist, if he has been able to weld them into a unity in his picture, they will add to the depth and value of the work of art.

By the subject of a picture we mean the life object or objects that were the starting point for the artist's creation of a work of art. Subject and meaning must be distinguished; they are two separate things. One might say that the subject of a picture is a framework about which the meaning can cling, but in all cases of great works of art the meaning transcends the subject in importance. The meaning of a picture touches us on so many levels of our consciousness, evokes so many buried emotional responses, stirs so many half-formed, unrecognized associations, that in many instances our response seems out of all proportion to the cause, which we mistakenly assume to be the subject. We have all probably felt this in relation to poetry, in which a few simple words touch a chord in us and evoke a response far greater than the subject of the poem seems to warrant. This is the magic of art. The subject or life object that starts the artist on his creative process is simply the match that starts the train of gunpowder ending in the fireworks display. The match itself is not the fireworks and disappears in the final result.

Every artist is started by something different; he funnels his emotion toward all of existence into a symbol standing for one object. We have already mentioned Van Gogh's shoes, in which he saw and expressed a broad, universal significance. Sincerity, belief, and genuine emotion are necessary in the artist in order to evoke belief in the spectator, and without belief no emotion is possible. The artist cannot communicate what

154

he has not lived in the interior life. His experience must be a real, valid emotional experience or it is a make-believe easily seen through. Real emotional experience may be purely imaginative in details, but it must be a logical unity, creating a new world, incongruous and illogical in the light of the real world, but logical and unified in view of the premises laid down by the artist.

This seems to be straying away from the question of subject, but it is to point out the fact that the life object from which the artist starts off on his creative way, the subject of the picture, is and must be completely irrelevant in the finished picture. We cannot repeat this too often, because to many people the basis of judgment for a work of art is its likeness to life. We know by now that a work of art is a new thing with a life of its own and must be evaluated by its own standards and laws. It is purely subjective and lives only in the minds of the spectators. For this reason art and the artist cannot exist without you, and we come back to the point that if art is to develop in the United States, you and I must develop. The public and the artist are inseparable; art can only thrive where there is an understanding between them.

It is not too easy to develop a real appreciation of art. If a work of art could be judged on labels, critical appraisal would be simple; all pictures of cows are good, or all cubist pictures are good. A logical-minded scientist, after seeking for underlying principles in art analogous to the definite classifications used in his science, baffled and frustrated at not finding them, decided, humorously, that all pictures with a spot of red in the lower left-hand corner were henceforth good to him. This made his judgments quick and simple. But the appreciation of art is a much more subtle thing.

The experience of enjoying a picture is like loving a person. That person cannot be classified; the sum of his or her qualities does not explain our feeling as a mathematical problem gives a certain answer. The difficulty is that the whole is infinitely greater than the parts. An analysis of a loved one feature by feature is futile; the whole personality gives the effect. And so it is with pictures; each work of art is superlative and unique, incomparable in quality to another. An analysis of its parts and techniques will never explain why we love it. Each work of art you look at must be the only one in the world for you for the time being. You must look at it with complete absorption, with no thought of another. But this state of being in love, this rapt absorption with the picture, cannot endure for long periods at a time. Eventually, of course, judgment steps in, and then our *real* experience with that picture is over temporarily. We can never wholly succeed in the analysis of a painting, but the attempt is the basis for a greater understanding and one of the possible ways of growth. If the picture is a worthy one, this rapt feeling that we have compared to being in love will return every time we see the picture again after an absence from it and will endure for longer or shorter periods.

We have said that after the first rapture, judgment steps in. Even this contributes to our pleasure in art; in fact, everything we are contributes to this pleasure, even memory and knowledge. It is impossible for us to regard anything long without passing a judgment on it consciously or unconsciously. Everything the mind perceives is fitted into a category of like things and compared to other known examples. Our standards are highly personalized, founded on our own former experiences. However, we are all human beings and the workings of our minds are similar; our judgments operate along the same lines, but the results differ as the experience and personality differ. This difference in personality and experience explains why we like one thing when we are young and another

156

when we are old. Our experience and personality change with the years. It explains why Mr. B. prefers Giotto and Mr. A. prefers Tintoretto. But there is a basic similarity in our judgments, and we find that we belong to a more or less large group of like-minded people in our tastes. To compare art appreciation again with the experience of love, our experience is unique and subjective; it takes place strictly within ourselves; no one can truly share our feeling. But nearly everyone falls in love and follows a pattern of falling in love, and a certain large group of people will even fall in love with the same type of person.

As you persist in your association with pictures, your ideals will change, the types of pictures to which you respond with love will vary, just as a man of twenty will need as friends more mature types of people than he loved at fifteen. As we mature in art, our tastes and needs change. If at the end of six months you find your taste in pictures the same as it was at the beginning of your exercises in art appreciation, you may deduce that something is wrong with the methods of development you have been using. If you are still persuaded that an understanding and appreciation of art will enrich your life, you should try to work out a system of art education for yourself suited to your own character and needs. But keep at it, keep associating with pictures. We do not consider the time wasted when we spend a few minutes a day for a year to learn to type or to speak French, and the personal rewards to be gained from that much time devoted to the study of pictures is incomparably greater.

We have tried to make clear that art is not an exact science. Even the technical aspect of art, its laws and traditions, have been evolved after the fact; that is, artists have painted their pictures and then teachers, critics, and aesthetes have attempted to discover why these pictures moved them and to

157

formulate rules. Every time a great artist lives and works, these rules must be changed to fit his new techniques and points of view. Like psychology, art is not an abstract, logical theory, but a pattern of the knowledge of men's minds based on observation of the mind itself. The laws of psychology are established from the study of the minds of many men; they are not a set of standards contrived in the abstract and then applied to men's minds like a yardstick. In both psychology and art our rules change as our knowledge increases. They change to include new data based on new personalities as they appear. All valid aesthetic principles must be broad and abstract enough not to interfere with novelty and creation. Broad principles of art have been reached by trial and error in experience and experiment by men through the ages. Restrictive rules have been applied to art and broken and discarded by artists, a process which is still going on. Only principles that are broad and basic remain.

It is fitting to link psychology and art here. The psychologists are discovering, in their excursions into men's minds, the deep-seated need for art. We have all been tinged with Puritanism in our upbringing, a long-lasting hangover from our early history. Puritanism teaches that pleasure not only does not justify itself but is actually harmful to the soul. Psychology now is proving that the pleasures provided by art satisfy needs in us that must be satisfied for the health and productivity of the individual and therefore of society, which is composed of individuals. Art adds to our understanding of life as a whole and therefore leads to greater freedom and wisdom in our choices and activities of daily life, in a better adaptation to our human environment. Freely creative art provides an insight into the whole of life. Enlargement of the spirit by art may affect all spheres of a man's life. In our education a one-sided emphasis on work rather than play, on industry rather

158

than leisure, on success rather than happiness, causes our ultimate lack of appreciation of the arts. The feeling of unity and of the possibility of perfection that art gives us may be carried over into life as a valuable feeling tone tinging our whole attitude to life. Art gives us a reaffirmation of life as orderly and beautiful.

The spectator attitude that we are trying to develop toward pictures may be developed toward life itself. We may succeed in regarding life detached and whole, unrelated to self or selfish interests. One can come to accept life with a passionate love and interest free from pride and ambition, with free and imaginative appreciation. Art develops our responses of curiosity, sympathy, wonder, and understanding. Artists have discovered the beauty values of life and shown us where and how to look. We can see the world through their eyes. Silently and unobtrusively art transforms the "background of values from which action springs." * The beliefs and sentiments that art imparts become a part of our nature. Art does not inspire any particular act but so molds our minds that every act is influenced. Cézanne wrote, "Art, I believe, puts us in the state of grace when universal emotion reveals itself to us, religiously, yet very naturally." "All art is great and good and true only in so far as it is distinctively the work of *manhood* in its highest sense—that is to say not the work of limbs and fingers, but of the soul. . . . By work of the soul I mean the reader always to understand the work of the entire immortal creature, proceeding from a quick, perceptive, and eager heart, perfected by the intellect, and finally dealt with by the hands, under the direct guidance of higher powers," said Ruskin.

* De Witt Parker, *op. cit.*

INDEX

A

Abell, Walter, 82
Abstract art, 19, 23
  psychological need for, 99
Abstraction, 19, 97–98, 114–116, 120
Activity, art, 17
Africa, 13
Alexander the Great, 8
Altamira, 17
America, children of, 47
American art, 11, 127
American scene, 136
Arabesques, 142
Arabs, 6
Arch, broken, 10
Architecture, English, 7
  Romanesque and Norman, 9
Armory Show, 107
Arnheim, Rudolf, 97
Art, applied, 141
  children's, 44
  definition of, 14
  equivocal, 41

Breughel's "Country Fair," 74
Buttress, flying, 10
Byzantine art, 8–9, 12

C

Camera, invention of the, 121
Career, art as a, 58
Catechism of the spectator, 130ff
Central Africa, children of, 47
Central America, 13
Cézanne, Paul, 99, 102–103, 115, 159
    use of colored planes by, 104
Chiaroscuro, 12
Children, artistic talent of, 48–53
Chinese art, 6–7, 12, 68
Chinese sculpture, 7
Christian art, 8
Christianity, 5, 8
Classicists, 100
Color, 80–85
    Cézanne's use of, 103
    cold, 86
    harmony of, 74, 143
    heightening of, 72
    local, 101
    in spatial orientation, 119
    tones of, 74
    use of, 121
    warm, 86
Color perspective, 117
Color prints, 126
Color scales, 74
Composition, axis of, 119
Concept, 70
Constantinople, 9
Constructivism, 95, 114
Content, emotional, 27
Contrast, 80, 143

164

Mondrian, Pieter, 113
Monet, Claude, 3
Moore, Henry, 115
"Morning," sonata called, 30–32
Movement, 83
  in futurist painting, 106
Movements in art, 4–5
  modern, 99–113
Muller Frienfels, Richard, 130n
Music, 29–30
Mystics, visions of, 77

N

Negro sculpture, 108
Neoplasticism, 95, 112
Nonobjectivism, 95
Nonrealistic art of children, 44
Nonrepresentational art, 115
Norman architecture, 9
North Africa, 6
"Nude Descending a Staircase," 107

O

Organization, systemic, 25
Orphism, 95

P

Pacific Islands, 13
Painting, abstraction in, 97–99
  cubism in, 104–105
  impressionist, 99–102
  influence of photography on, 96, 106–107
  perspective in, 80–81
  realism in, 18–21
  standards of beauty in, 15, 28, 37
  surrealist, 109–111